"I'd bet the farm that no family has ever been as unhappy in as many ways—and to such sensationally entertaining effect—as the Westons of *August: Osage County*, a fraught, densely plotted saga of an Oklahoma clan in a state of near-apocalyptic meltdown. Fiercely funny and bitingly sad, this turbo-charged tragicomedy—which spans three acts and more than three blissful hours—doesn't just jump-start the fall theater season, *August* throws it instantaneously into high gear."

—CHARLES ISHERWOOD, *New York Times*

"The best new play to emerge from Chicago in at least a generation."

—CHRIS JONES, *Chicago Tribune*

"The new Broadway season's first must-see offering. This is a play that will leave us laughing and wondering, shuddering and smiling, long after the house lights come back on."

—ROB KENDT, *Newsday*

"*August* is Letts's vision of the American family writ large—geographically scattered yet incestuously close, and destined to move through the world all alone."

—HEDY WEISS, *Chicago Sun-Times*

"In Tracy Letts's ferociously entertaining play, the American dysfunctional family drama comes roaring into the twenty-first century with eyes blazing, nostrils flaring and fangs bared, laced with corrosive humor so darkly delicious and ghastly that you're squirming in your seat even as you're doubled-over laughing. A massive meditation on the cruel realities that often belie standard expectations of conjugal and family accord—not to mention on the decline of American integrity itself."

—DAVID ROONEY, *Variety*

AUGUST:
OSAGE COUNTY

❋

AUGUST:
OSAGE COUNTY

TRACY LETTS

THEATRE COMMUNICATIONS GROUP
NEW YORK

August: Osage County is published by Theatre Communications Group, Inc., 520 Eighth Avenue, 24th Floor, New York, NY 10018-4156

This publication is made possible in part with public funds from the New York State Council on the Arts, a State Agency.

TCG books are exclusively distributed to the book trade by Consortium Book Sales and Distribution.

LIBRARY OF CONGRESS CATALOGING-IN-PUBLICATION DATA

Letts, Tracy, 1965–
August: Osage County / by Tracy Letts.
p. cm.
ISBN 978-1-55936-466-9
ISBN 978-1-55936-609-0 (ebook)
1. Family—Drama. 2. Husband and wife—Drama. 3. Parent and adult child—Drama. 4. Oklahoma—Drama. 5. Domestic drama. 6. Tragicomedy.
I. Title.
PS3612.E887A75 2007
812'.6—dc22 2007051952

Text design and composition by Lisa Govan
Cover art © 2013 by The Weinstein Company

First Edition, January 2008
New Edition, October 2013

For Dad

✳

ACKNOWLEDGMENTS

Anna Shapiro.

Martha Lavey, David Hawkanson, Erica Daniels, Steppenwolf Theatre Company.

Jeffrey Richards, Jean Doumanian, Steve Traxler, Jerry Frankel.

Ian Barford, Deanna Dunagan, Kimberly Guerrero, Francis Guinan, Fawn Johnstin, Brian Kerwin, Dennis Letts, Madeleine Martin, Mariann Mayberry, Amy Morton, Sally Murphy, Jeff Perry, Rondi Reed, Rick Snyder, Troy West.

Ed Sobel, Todd Rosenthal, Annie Wrightson, Ana Kuzmanic, Richard Woodbury, David Singer, Deb Styer, Michelle Medvin.

Brant Russell, Mike Nussbaum, Sadieh Rifai, Penny Slusher, John Judd, Jeff Still, Katie Crawford, Lauren Katz, David Pasquesi, Mike Shannon, David Cromer, Henry Wishcamper.

Howard Starks, my late mentor. For the poem "August: Osage County."

Nicole Wiesner, all my love.

Shawn and Shari, Dana and Deborah.

Billie Letts, Barbara Santee, Dewey Dougless. Your fortitude is a marvel.

Bill and Virginia Gipson. With love and letting go.

AUGUST:
OSAGE COUNTY

✳

PRODUCTION HISTORY

August: Osage County premiered in June 2007 at Steppenwolf Theatre Company (Martha Lavey, Artistic Director; David Hawkanson, Executive Director) in Chicago. The director was Anna D. Shapiro; the scenic designer was Todd Rosenthal, the costume designer was Ana Kuzmanic, the lighting designer was Ann G. Wrightson, the sound designer was Richard Woodbury; original music was composed by David Singer, fight choreography was by Chuck Coyl, casting was by Erica Daniels; the dramaturg was Edward Sobel, the dialect coach was Cecilie O'Reilly, the stage manager was Deb Styer and the assistant stage manager was Michelle Medvin. The cast was as follows:

BEVERLY WESTON	Dennis Letts
VIOLET WESTON	Deanna Dunagan
BARBARA FORDHAM	Amy Morton
BILL FORDHAM	Jeff Perry
JEAN FORDHAM	Fawn Johnstin
IVY WESTON	Sally Murphy
KAREN WESTON	Mariann Mayberry
MATTIE FAE AIKEN	Rondi Reed
CHARLIE AIKEN	Francis Guinan
LITTLE CHARLES AIKEN	Ian Barford
JOHNNA MONEVATA	Kimberly Guerrero
STEVE HEIDEBRECHT	Rick Snyder
SHERIFF DEON GILBEAU	Troy West

August: Osage County opened on Broadway at the Imperial Theatre on December 4, 2007. It was produced by Jeffrey Richards, Jean Doumanian, Steve Traxler, Jerry Frankel, Ostar Productions, Jennifer Manocherian, The Weinstein Company, Debra Black, Daryl Roth, Ronald Frankel, Marc Frankel, Barbara Freitag and Phil Mickelson, and Rick Steiner and Staton Bell Group. The cast and artistic team were the same, except for the following changes: additional casting was provided by Stuart Howard, Amy Schecter and Paul Hardt; and casting changes were:

JEAN FORDHAM   Madeleine Martin
STEVE HEIDEBRECHT   Brian Kerwin

CHARACTERS

The Weston Family:

BEVERLY WESTON, sixty-nine years old
VIOLET WESTON, Bev's wife, sixty-five years old

BARBARA FORDHAM, Bev and Violet's daughter, forty-six
years old
BILL FORDHAM, her husband, forty-nine years old
JEAN FORDHAM, their daughter, fourteen years old

IVY WESTON, Bev and Violet's daughter, forty-four years old

KAREN WESTON, Bev and Violet's daughter, forty years old

MATTIE FAY AIKEN, Violet's sister, fifty-seven years old
CHARLIE AIKEN, Mattie Fay's husband, sixty years old
LITTLE CHARLES AIKEN, their son, thirty-seven years old

Others:

JOHNNA MONEVATA, housekeeper, twenty-six years old
STEVE HEIDEBRECHT, Karen's fiancé, fifty years old
SHERIFF DEON GILBEAU, forty-seven years old

SETTING

August 2007.
 A large country home outside Pawhuska, Oklahoma, sixty miles northwest of Tulsa.

The child comes home and the parent puts the hooks in him. The old man, or the woman, as the case may be, hasn't got anything to say to the child. All he wants is to have that child sit in a chair for a couple of hours and then go off to bed under the same roof. It's not love. I am not saying that there is not such a thing as love. I am merely pointing to something which is different from love but which sometimes goes by the name of love. It may well be that without this thing which I am talking about there would not be any love. But this thing in itself is not love. It is just something in the blood. It is a kind of blood greed, and it is the fate of a man. It is the thing which man has which distinguishes him from the happy brute creation. When you get born your father and mother lost something out of themselves, and they are going to bust a hame trying to get it back, and you are it. They know they can't get it all back but they will get as big a chunk out of you as they can. And the good old family reunion, with picnic dinner under the maples, is very much like diving into the octopus tank at the aquarium.

—ROBERT PENN WARREN, *All the King's Men*

PROLOGUE

A rambling country house outside Pawhuska, Oklahoma, sixty miles northwest of Tulsa. More than a century old, the house was probably built by a clan of successful Irish homesteaders. Additions, renovations and repairs have essentially modernized the house until 1972 or so, when all structural care ceased.

The First Floor:

The three main playing areas are separated by entryways. Stage-right, the dining room. The Mission-style table seats eight; the matching sideboard holds the fine china. A tatty crystal-tiered chandelier hangs over the table and casts a gloomy yellow light. An archway upstage leads to a sitting room. A rotary-dial telephone rests on a small side table, beside an upholstered chair. Further upstage, a doorway leads to a hallway, off.

Downstage-center, the living room. Hide-a-bed, TV, hi-fi turntable, Wurlitzer electric piano.

Left, the study. A medium-sized desk is piled with books, legal pads, manila folders, notepaper. An archway upstage leads to the

*house's front door, landing, and a stairway to the second floor.
Further upstage, a doorway opens onto a partial view of the kitchen.*

*Far left, the front porch, strewn with dead grass and a few
rolled-up small-town newspapers.*

The Second Floor:

*The stairway arrives at a landing (above the sitting room on the
first floor). A cushioned window seat, a hallway leading to the bed-
rooms, off, and another stairway leading to . . .*

The Attic:

*A single chamber, center, with peaked roof and slanted walls,
inexpensively modeled into a bedroom.*

The house is filled with books.

*All the windows in the house have been covered with cheap
plastic shades. Black duct tape seals the edge of the shades, effect-
ing a complete absence of outside light.*

*Lit dimly by his desk lamp, Beverly Weston, drunk, nurses a
glass of whiskey as he "interviews" Johnna Monevata.*

BEVERLY: "Life is very long . . ."

T. S. Eliot. I mean . . . he's given credit for it because he
bothered to write it down. He's not the first person to say
it . . . certainly not the first person to think it. *Feel* it. But
he wrote the words on a sheet of paper and signed it and
the four-eyed prick was a genius . . . so if you say it, you
have to say his name after it.

"Life is very long": T. S. Eliot.

Absolutely goddamn right. Especially in his case, since
he lived to be seventy-six or something, a very long life,
especially in those days. And he was only in his thirties
when he wrote it so he must've had some inside dope.

Give the devil his due. Very few poets could've made it
through his . . . his trial and come out on the other side,
brilliantined and double-breasted and Anglican. Not hard
to imagine, faced with Eliot's first wife, lovely Viv, how Hart
Crane or John Berryman might've reacted, just foot-raced
to the nearest bridge, Olympian Suicidalists. Not Eliot: fol-

lowing sufficient years of ecclesiastical guilt, plop her in the nearest asylum and get on with the day. God a-mighty. You have to admire the purity of the survivor's instinct.

Berryman, the old goat: "The world is gradually becoming a place where I do not care to be anymore." I don't know what it says about me that I have a greater affinity with the damaged. Probably nothing good. I admire the hell out of Eliot *the poet*, but the *person*? I can't identify.

VIOLET *(Offstage)*: . . . son-of-a-bitch . . .

BEVERLY: Violet. My wife. She takes pills, sometimes a great many. And they affect . . . among other things, her equilibrium. Fortunately, the pills she takes eliminate her *need* for equilibrium. So she falls when she rambles . . . but she doesn't ramble much.

My wife takes pills and I drink. That's the bargain we've struck . . . *one* of the bargains, just one paragraph of our marriage contract . . . cruel covenant. She takes pills and I drink. I don't drink *because* she takes pills. As to whether she takes pills because I drink . . . I learned long ago not to speak for my wife. The reasons why we partake are anymore inconsequential. The facts are: my wife takes pills and I drink. And these facts have over time made burdensome the maintenance of traditional American routine: paying of bills, purchase of goods, cleaning of clothes or carpets or crappers. Rather than once more assume the mantle of guilt . . . vow abstinence with my fingers crossed in the queasy hope of righting our ship, I've chosen to turn my life over to a Higher Power . . . *(Hoists his glass)* . . . and join the ranks of the Hiring Class.

It's not a decision with which I'm entirely comfortable. I know how to launder my dirty undies . . . done it all my life, me or my wife, but I'm finding it's getting in the way of my drinking. "Something has been said for sobriety but very little." (Berryman again.) And now you are here.

The place isn't in such bad shape, not yet. I've done all right. I've managed. And just last night, I burned an awful lot of . . . debris . . .

Y'know . . . a simple utility bill can mean so much to a living person. Once they've passed, though . . . after they've passed, the words and numbers just seem like . . . otherworldly symbols. It's only paper. Worse. Worse than blank paper.

(Johnna wipes sweat from her brow. Beverly takes a folded handkerchief from his pocket and hands it to her.)

This is clean.

JOHNNA *(Wiping her forehead)*: Thank you.

BEVERLY: I apologize for the temperature in here. My wife is cold-blooded and not just in the metaphorical sense. She does not believe in air-conditioning . . . as if it is a thing to be disbelieved.

JOHNNA: My daddy was the same way. I'm used to it.

BEVERLY: I knew Mr. Youngbird, you know.

JOHNNA: You knew Daddy?

BEVERLY: Small town. Bought many a watermelon from his fruit stand. Some summers he sold fireworks too, right?

JOHNNA: Yes, sir.

BEVERLY: I bought roman candles for my children. He did pass, didn't he?

JOHNNA: Yes, sir.

BEVERLY: May I ask how?

JOHNNA: He had a heart attack. Fell into a flatbed truck full of wine grapes.

BEVERLY: Wine grapes. In Oklahoma. I'm sorry.

JOHNNA: Thank you.

(He finishes his drink, pours another.)

BEVERLY: May I ask about the name?

JOHNNA: Hm?

BEVERLY: He was Youngbird and you are . . .

JOHNNA: Monevata.

BEVERLY: "Monevata."

JOHNNA: I went back to the original language.
BEVERLY: And does it mean "young bird"?
JOHNNA: Yes.
BEVERLY: And taking the name, that was your choice?
JOHNNA: Mm-hm.
BEVERLY *(Raising his glass)*: Cheers.

(Violet calls from offstage.)

VIOLET *(Offstage)*: Bev . . . ?

BEVERLY *(To himself)*:
    By night within that ancient house
    Immense, black, damned, anonymous.

(Lights up, dimly, on the second-floor landing. Just out of bed, wearing wrinkled clothes, smoking a Winston, Violet squints down the darkened stairway.)

VIOLET: Bev!
BEVERLY: Yes?
VIOLET: Did you pullish . . . ?
BEVERLY: What?
VIOLET: Did you . . .

(Long pause. Violet stares, waiting for an answer. Beverly stares, waiting for her to complete her question.)

BEVERLY: What, dear?
VIOLET: Oh, goddamn it . . . did. You. Are the police here?
BEVERLY: No.
VIOLET: Is this a window? Am I looking through window? A window?
BEVERLY: Can you come here?

(Violet considers, then clomps down the stairs, into the study, nonplussed by Johnna.)

VIOLET: Oh. *(Vaguely)* Hello.

JOHNNA: Hello.

VIOLET *(To Beverly)*: I didn't know you were entertaaaaaaining.

BEVERLY: This is Johnna, the young woman I told you about.

VIOLET: You're tell me's a woman.

BEVERLY: Pardon?

VIOLET: A woman. Wo-man. Whoa-man.

BEVERLY: Yes, dear, the young woman I'm hiring. To watch the place.

VIOLET: Oh! You're hiring women's now the thing. I thought you meant the other woman.

BEVERLY: What other woman?

VIOLET *(Pause; then, ugly)*: Huh?!

BEVERLY: I hope to hire her to cook and clean and take you to the clinic and to the—

VIOLET *(Attempting to over-articulate)*: In the int'rest of . . . civil action . . . your par-tic-u-lars ways of speak-king, I thought you meant you had thought a whoa-man to be HIRED!

BEVERLY: I don't understand you.

VIOLET *(Suddenly winsome, to Johnna)*: Hello.

JOHNNA: Hello.

VIOLET: I'm sorry. *(Curtsies)* Like this.

JOHNNA: Yes, ma'am.

VIOLET: I'm Violet. What's your name?

JOHNNA: Johnna.

VIOLET: You're very pretty.

JOHNNA: Thank you.

VIOLET: Are you an Indian?

JOHNNA: Yes, ma'am.

VIOLET: What kind?

JOHNNA: Cheyenne.

VIOLET: Do you think I'm pretty?

JOHNNA: Yes, ma'am.

VIOLET *(Curtsies again)*: Like . . . this? *(Curtsies again)* Like this . . . *(Curtsies lower, stumbles, catches herself)*

BEVERLY: Careful.

VIOLET *(Still to Johnna)*: You're the house now. I'm sorry, I . . . I took some medicine for my musssss . . . muscular.

BEVERLY: Why don't you go back to bed, sweetheart?

VIOLET: Why don't you go fuck a fucking sow's ass?

BEVERLY: All right.

VIOLET *(To Johnna)*: I'm sorry. I'll be sickly sweet. I'm soooooooooooo sweet. In-el-abrially sweet.

(She stubs out her cigarette on Beverly's desk ashtray . . . stares at Johnna as if she might say something else . . . then suddenly exits.)

BEVERLY: I think I mentioned on the phone that Dr. Burke recommended you. He feels you're qualified to handle the needs of our household.

JOHNNA: I have a year toward my nursing certificate at Tulsa Community College, but I had to drop out when Daddy died. And I saw my mom and grandma through bad times.

BEVERLY: Dr. Burke says you've been struggling for work.

JOHNNA: I've been cleaning houses and babysitting.

BEVERLY: He did tell you we wanted a live-in.

JOHNNA: Yes, sir.

BEVERLY: We keep unusual hours here. Try not to differentiate between night and day. I doubt you'll be able to maintain any sort of a healthy routine.

JOHNNA: I need the work.

BEVERLY: The work itself . . . pretty mundane. I myself require very little personal attention. Thrive without it, in fact, sort of a human cactus. My *wife* has been diagnosed with a touch of cancer, so she'll need to be driven to Tulsa for her final chemotherapy treatments. You're welcome to use that American-made behemoth parked in the carport. You're welcome to make use of anything, everything, all this garbage we've acquired, our life's work. If you're going to live here, I want you to live here. You understand?

JOHNNA: Yes, sir.

BEVERLY: Please call me Beverly. Do you have any questions?

JOHNNA: What kind of cancer?

BEVERLY: I didn't say? My God, I nearly neglected the punch line: *mouth* cancer.

JOHNNA: What pills does she take?

BEVERLY: Valium. Vicodin. Darvon, Darvocet. Percodan, Percocet. Xanax for fun. OxyContin in a pinch. Some Black Mollies once, just to make sure I was still paying attention. And of course Dilaudid. I shouldn't forget Dilaudid.

(Beverly studies her. Finishes his drink.)

My wife. Violet. Violet, my wife, doesn't believe she needs treatment for her habit. She has been down that road once before, and came out of it clean as a whistle . . . then chose for herself this reality instead.

You were about to ask why she isn't currently seeking treatment. Weren't you?

JOHNNA: No, sir.

BEVERLY: Oh, good, that relieves me. Now hold on a second . . .

(Beverly wobbles to his feet unsteadily, as much from weariness as drink, explores his bookshelf.)

My last refuge, my books: simple pleasures, like finding wild onions by the side of a road, or requited love.

(He takes a book from his bookshelf and gives it to Johnna.)

JOHNNA: T. S. Eliot.

BEVERLY: Read it or not. It isn't a job requirement. That's just for your enjoyment. Feel free to read any of my books.

  Here we go round the prickly pear
  Prickly pear prickly pear
  Here we go round the prickly pear . . .

ACT ONE

SCENE 1

Ivy, Mattie Fae and Charlie are in the living room. Mattie Fae drinks a glass of scotch. Charlie has the TV tuned to a baseball game, the sound low, and he keeps an eye on the score as he nurses a bottle of beer.

Elsewhere in the house: Violet talks on the telephone in the sitting room; Johnna cooks and cleans in the kitchen.

MATTIE FAE: Beverly's done this before.

IVY: I know.

MATTIE FAE: You remember he used to just take off, no call, nothing. You remember, Charlie?

CHARLIE: They've always had trouble—

MATTIE FAE: One time, this one time, he just up and left without a word, I told Vi, I said, "You pack that son-of-a-bitch's bags and have them waiting for him on the *front porch.*" And you know I always liked your father.

IVY: I know.

MATTIE FAE: No, I always liked your father, you know that. I introduced Vi and Bev, for God's sake.

CHARLIE: You did not introduce them.

MATTIE FAE: The hell I didn't.

CHARLIE: You had a date with him and stood him up and sent your sister instead.

MATTIE FAE: *That's an introduction.* That's what an introduction is.

CHARLIE: I just don't think it's accurate to say—

MATTIE FAE: He was too old for me and anyway, Violet? "Shrinking Violet?" She couldn't meet a man on her own.

CHARLIE: No one ever called her "Shrinking Violet"—

MATTIE FAE: And Charlie and your father always got on real well. They used to go on fishing trips together.

IVY: I know.

MATTIE FAE: But when Beverly just took off like that, without saying anything, without a note even, my first obligation was to look after my sister, don'tcha know.

CHARLIE: You don't have an obligation to do anything.

MATTIE FAE: I have an obligation to look after my sister.

CHARLIE: You're not obliged to get involved in somebody else's marriage.

MATTIE FAE: Not any marriage, but when they're married to my big sister, I sure as hell do. Ivy has sisters, she knows what I mean. I told her, I said, "Vi, you pack that son-of-a-bitch's bags and put them on the front porch. You take all those goddamn books he's so fond of and you make a big pile in the front yard and you have yourself a bonfire. Take all his papers too, just everything and throw it in—"

CHARLIE: You don't burn a man's books.

MATTIE FAE: Will you stop? You keep contradicting—

CHARLIE: The man's books didn't do anything. His possessions aren't responsible.

MATTIE FAE: Well, she didn't do it, so it doesn't make any—

CHARLIE: Of course she didn't do it.

MATTIE FAE: Let me tell you something, Charlie Aiken: you ever get any ideas about just up and taking off, you better believe—

CHARLIE: I'm not going anywhere—

MATTIE FAE: I'm saying if you did, you better believe I'm gonna give you about three days to get your head straight and then it's all going up in a blaze of glory.

CHARLIE: I'm not going anywhere!

MATTIE FAE: If you did!

CHARLIE: I'm not!

MATTIE FAE: Not that Charlie has any books lying around. I don't think I've ever seen Charlie read a book in my life.

CHARLIE: Is that a criticism? Does that bother you?

MATTIE FAE: Well, I haven't. What's the last book you read?

CHARLIE: Goddamn it—

MATTIE FAE: Just tell me the last book you read.

CHARLIE: Beverly was a teacher; teachers read books. I'm in the upholstery business; people in the upholstery business—

MATTIE FAE: You can't tell me the last book you read.

CHARLIE: This girl is concerned about her daddy's whereabouts. She doesn't need to sit here and listen to us—

MATTIE FAE: I think we're all concerned about Beverly.

CHARLIE: Then what the hell are you needling me for?

MATTIE FAE: He came back though, you know, and they worked things out, and he'll come back again, I know he will.

IVY: I think this time is different.

MATTIE FAE: I think so too.

CHARLIE: Why?

MATTIE FAE: Because back then—

CHARLIE: I'm not asking you. *(To Ivy)* Why do you think this time is different?

IVY: Because I think back then they were trying.

MATTIE FAE *(To Charlie)*: Which is what I was gonna say. *(To Ivy)* Beverly was a very complicated man.

IVY: I know.

CHARLIE: Stop saying "was."

MATTIE FAE: Well, he was. He is, very complicated.

CHARLIE: But in a kind-y quiet way.

IVY: Kind of like Charles.

CHARLIE: Yes, like Little Charles. Exactly—

MATTIE FAE: Oh. He's nothing like Little Charles.

CHARLIE: She just means in their sort of quiet complicated ways—

MATTIE FAE: Little Charles isn't complicated.

CHARLIE: I think—

MATTIE FAE: No, Little Charles isn't complicated, he's just unemployed.

CHARLIE: He's an observer.

MATTIE FAE: All he observes is the television.

CHARLIE: So you can't even see Ivy's point?

MATTIE FAE: No.

CHARLIE: That Little Charles and Beverly share some kind of . . . complication.

MATTIE FAE: Honey, you have to be smart to be complicated.

CHARLIE: That's our boy. Are you saying our boy isn't smart?

MATTIE FAE: Yes, that's what I'm saying.

CHARLIE: What's the matter with you? *(To Ivy)* Your cousin is very smart.

MATTIE FAE: I'm sweating. Are you sweating?

CHARLIE: Hell, yes, I'm sweating, it's ninety degrees in here.

MATTIE FAE: Feel my back.

CHARLIE: I don't want to feel your back.

MATTIE FAE: Feel it. Sweat is just dripping down my back.

CHARLIE: I believe you.

MATTIE FAE: Feel it.

CHARLIE: No.

MATTIE FAE: Come on, put your hand here—

CHARLIE: Goddamn it—

MATTIE FAE: Sweat's just dripping—

CHARLIE: Ivy. Let me ask you something. When did this start? This business with the shades, taping the shades?

IVY: That's been a couple of years now.

MATTIE FAE: My gosh, has it been that long since we've been here?

CHARLIE: Do you know its purpose?

MATTIE FAE: You can't tell if it's night or day.

IVY: I think that's the purpose.

CHARLIE: Well, I don't know, but I don't think that's healthy.

MATTIE FAE: It's not. You need sunlight.

CHARLIE: Do you know which one of them decided on this?

IVY: I can't really see Dad taking the initiative.

CHARLIE: No, I suppose not. I don't know about you, but I find this whole setup depressing. Y'know, a person's *environment* . . . *(Points to the stereo)* And what the hell, is that an Eric Clapton album? Vi's a *Clapton fan?*

(Mattie Fae starts to peel the tape from one of the shades.)

Don't do that.

MATTIE FAE: The body needs sunlight.

CHARLIE: It's nighttime. And this isn't your place, you can't come into somebody else's home and start changing—

MATTIE FAE: Do you believe we haven't been here in two years?

(Violet enters.)

VIOLET: He said they checked the hospitals but no Beverly.

MATTIE FAE: This is the highway patrol?

VIOLET: No, not the highway patrol, the sheriff, the Gilbeau boy.

MATTIE FAE: Gilbeau. Don't tell me C. J. Gilbeau is the sheriff here now.

VIOLET: Not C. J., his boy Deon.

MATTIE FAE: I was gonna say—

VIOLET: He went to school with the girls, Deon did. Was he in your class, Ivy?

IVY: Barbara's class, I think.

MATTIE FAE: Is that right?

21

CHARLIE: Who's this now?

MATTIE FAE: C. J. Gilbeau was a boy we grew up with. Mean little son-of-a-bitch, juvenile delinquent—

VIOLET: His boy Deon's the sheriff now.

MATTIE FAE: C. J. was the preacher's son and you know—

CHARLIE: Say no more.

MATTIE FAE: —and you *know* how they are.

VIOLET: You remember he went to the penitentiary.

MATTIE FAE: Yes, I remember that, for killing what was it?

VIOLET: A boxer.

MATTIE FAE: Right, for killing this man's boxer dog.

VIOLET: His boy Deon's the sheriff. I sent you that subscription to the *Pawhuska Journal-Capital*. Don't you read it?

MATTIE FAE: No, I don't read it.

VIOLET: So you Tulsa big shots could keep up with us small-town folks.

MATTIE FAE: No, I don't read it.

VIOLET: Well, if you read it you'd know that his boy Deon is the sheriff here now.

IVY: What hospitals did they check?

VIOLET: He rattled off a bunch of them.

IVY: What else did he say?

VIOLET: The boat's missing.

(Pause.)

IVY: Mom?

VIOLET: He sent a patrolman out to the dock to check if anybody had seen him and Beverly's pontoon boat is gone.

MATTIE FAE: Oh, no.

VIOLET: He said they've had a couple of boats stolen in the last little while so he didn't think it proved anything, but he was worried about it.

(Violet starts to ascend the stairs.)

CHARLIE: Vi, you think there's a chance Bev loaded that boat onto his trailer and took it out of there? I mean if he was going somewhere's else.

MATTIE FAE: Trailer's out by the shed, I saw it when we pulled up.

(Violet exits. Ivy follows her. Johnna enters, occupied with housework. Charlie holds up his empty beer bottle.)

CHARLIE: 'Scuse me, dear . . . could I trouble you for another beer?

MATTIE FAE: Goddamn it, she's not a waitress.

CHARLIE: I know that.

MATTIE FAE: Then get your own beer.

(Johnna crosses, takes the empty . . .)

JOHNNA: I'll get it.

(. . . and goes.)

MATTIE FAE: I don't believe you. Watchin' the baseball game and drinkin' beers. Don't you have any sense of what's going on around you? This situation is fraught.

CHARLIE: Am I supposed to sit here like a statue? You're drinking whiskey.

MATTIE FAE: I'm having a cocktail.

CHARLIE: You're drinking straight whiskey.

MATTIE FAE: Just . . . show a little class.

CHARLIE: I don't think we need to sit here crying in the dark.

MATTIE FAE: Oh well, since you got everything all figured out, let's party down.

CHARLIE: Mattie Fae—

MATTIE FAE: Get that Indian gal to whip us up some cheese Coneys and let's call a few friends.

CHARLIE: Oooh, a cheese Coney sounds good.

MATTIE FAE: It does, doesn't it? You smell something cooking?
CHARLIE: Yeah.
MATTIE FAE: Come with me to the kitchen, let's see what it is.
CHARLIE: What do you need me for? I've got the Royals on.
MATTIE FAE: Just come with me.

(She takes his hand, pulls him from the couch.)

CHARLIE: That's not good news about that boat.

(As Charlie follows Mattie Fae to the kitchen, and intercepts his beer from Johnna, the lights crossfade to Violet and Ivy on the second-floor landing. During the following, they descend the stairs and enter the dining room.)

VIOLET: Did you call Barb?
IVY: Yes.
VIOLET: When'd you call her?
IVY: This morning.
VIOLET: What'd she say?
IVY: She's on her way.
VIOLET: How's she getting here?
IVY: She and Bill are coming.
VIOLET: Is she driving?
IVY: I doubt it.
VIOLET: Why?
IVY: Boulder's a long way.
VIOLET: Is she bringing Jean?
IVY: I don't know.
VIOLET: When did she say she'd be here?
IVY: She didn't say. She just said she was on her way.
VIOLET: What'd you tell her?
IVY: I told her Dad was missing.
VIOLET: That's all.
IVY: Is there anything else?
VIOLET: Did you tell her how long he'd been missing?

IVY: Five days.

VIOLET: Did you tell her that?

IVY: I think so.

VIOLET: What did she say?

IVY: She said she was on her way.

VIOLET: Goddamn it, Ivy, what did she *say*? Was she irritated? Was she amused? Tell me what she said.

IVY: She said she was on her way.

VIOLET: You're hopeless. *(Takes a pill)* Goddamn your father for putting me through this. For leaving me to handle this. You seen that office of his, all that paperwork, that mess? I can't make heads or tails of it. He hired this Indian a week ago to look after the place for some goddamn reason and now I have a stranger in my house. I don't know what to say to that girl. What's her name?

IVY: Johnna.

VIOLET: He's always paid the bills and made the phone calls and now suddenly I'm supposed to handle it? You know this house is falling apart, something about the basement or the sump pump or the foundation. I don't know anything about it. I can't do all this by myself.

IVY: I called Karen.

VIOLET: What did she say?

IVY: She said she'd try to get here.

VIOLET: She'll be a big fat help, just like you. *(Takes another pill)* I need Barb.

IVY: I don't know what Barb's going to be able to do.

VIOLET: What did you do to your hair?

IVY: I had it straightened.

VIOLET: You had it straightened. Why would anybody do that?

IVY: I don't know.

VIOLET: Why did *you* do it?

IVY: I just wanted a change.

VIOLET: You're a pretty girl. You're the prettiest of my three girls, but you always look like such a schlub. Why don't you wear any makeup?

IVY: Do I need makeup?

VIOLET: All women need makeup. Don't let anybody tell you different. The only woman who was pretty enough to go without makeup was Elizabeth Taylor and she wore a *ton*. Sit up straight.

IVY: Mom.

VIOLET: Your shoulders are slumped and your hair's all straight and you don't wear makeup. You look like a lesbian. You're a pretty enough girl you could get a decent man if you spruced up. A bit, that's all I'm saying.

IVY: I'm not looking for a man.

VIOLET: You should be. Everybody needs somebody.

IVY: I'm not looking for a man.

VIOLET: Listen, there are a lot of losers out there, don't think I don't know it. But just because you got a bad one doesn't mean—

IVY: Barry wasn't a loser.

VIOLET: Barry was an asshole. And I warned you from the start, didn't I? First time you brought him over here in his ridiculous little electric car, with that stupid orange beard and that turban.

IVY: It wasn't a turban—

VIOLET: I just don't understand some of the choices you make. You're forty-three years old—

IVY: Forty-four.

VIOLET: Forty-four years old. Maybe you're past the point of having children, and that's all right if you don't want them, but aren't you interested in finding a husband?

IVY: A husband. In *Pawhuska*.

VIOLET: You don't meet people where you live, you meet them where you work. You work at a college. Don't tell me there aren't people coming through the door of that library every day.

IVY: You want me to marry a student, some eighteen-year-old boy from one of these hick towns?

VIOLET: They still have teachers on the Tulsa campus, don't they? They did when your father taught there—

IVY: Barry was a teacher at TU.

VIOLET: Yeah, "Environmental Studies." Barry was a *loser*.

IVY: He wasn't a loser—

VIOLET: He dumped you, didn't he? To my mind, that makes him—

IVY: He did not dump me. It just didn't work out between us.

VIOLET: All right, yes, dear, I'm sorry. I'll get it straight. I'm sorry. But maybe it would've worked out between you if you'd worn some makeup. *(Takes another pill)* How many was that?

IVY: I wasn't counting.

(Violet takes another pill.)

Is your mouth burning?

VIOLET: Like a son-of-a-bitch. My tongue is on fire.

IVY: Are you supposed to be smoking?

VIOLET: Is anybody supposed to smoke?

IVY: You have cancer of the mouth.

VIOLET: Ivy. I have enough to worry about right this minute without you getting on me about my smoking.

IVY: I'm not getting on you.

VIOLET: Just leave it alone.

IVY: Are you scared?

VIOLET: 'Course I'm scared. And you are a comfort, sweetheart. Thank God one of my girls stayed close to home. My generation, families stayed together.

IVY: That was a different time.

VIOLET: No kidding. Did you call Mattie Fae?

IVY: Aunt Mattie Fae's here.

VIOLET: I know that, dummy, did *you* call her?

IVY: I thought you called her.

VIOLET: I guess I did. I don't remember.

IVY: You've got a lot on your mind.

VIOLET: She means to come in here and tell *me* what's what.

IVY: I don't know how Uncle Charlie puts up with it.

VIOLET: He smokes a lot of grass.
IVY: He does?
VIOLET: He smokes a *lot* of grass.

(They laugh.)

IVY: "Grass"? You say "grass"?
VIOLET: What do you call it?
IVY: Hey, are you into Clapton now?
VIOLET: What?
IVY: Eric Clapton, you have an Eric Clapton album.
VIOLET: I've had it forever.
IVY: I've never seen it.
VIOLET: I like it. It's got a good beat. I'm not old, you know.

(Lights down on the dining room and up on the front porch as Barbara and Bill arrive, carrying suitcases. Violet and Ivy exit and, during the following, Mattie Fae and Charlie enter from the kitchen and cross to the dining room with plates of hot apple pie.)

BARBARA: What's Jean doing?
BILL: Smoking.
BARBARA: I wish you wouldn't encourage that.
BILL: I haven't encouraged anything.
BARBARA: I don't know, there's just something a little funny about the way you say, "smoking," like you admire her for getting hooked at fourteen.
BILL: Are you ready for this?
BARBARA: No. No way.
BILL: Well. Take a second.

(They stand, taking in the night, breathing the air.)

BARBARA: Goddamn, it's hot.
BILL: Wimp.

BARBARA: I know it. Colorado spoiled me.

BILL: That's one of the reasons we got out of here.

BARBARA: No, it's not.

BILL: You suppose your mom's turned on the air conditioner?

BARBARA: Are you kidding? Remember the parakeets?

BILL: The parakeets.

BARBARA: I didn't tell you about the parakeets? She got a parakeet, for some insane reason, and the little fucker croaked after about two days. So she went to the pet store and raised hell and they gave her another parakeet. That one died after just one day. So she went back and they gave her a third parakeet and that one died, too. So the chick from the pet store came out here to see just what in hell this serial parakeet killer was doing to bump off these birds.

BILL: And?

BARBARA: The heat. It was too hot. They were dying from the heat.

BILL: Jesus.

BARBARA: These are tropical birds, all right? They live in the fucking tropics.

(Beat. She looks out.)

What were these people thinking?

BILL: What people?

BARBARA: The jokers who settled this place. The Germans and the Dutch and the Irish. Who was the asshole who saw this flat hot nothing and planted his flag? I mean, we fucked the Indians for *this*?

BILL: Well, genocide always seems like such a good idea *at the time.*

BARBARA: Right, you need a little hindsight.

BILL: Anyway, if you want me to explain the creepy character of the Midwest, you're asking the wrong—

BARBARA: Hey. Please. This is not the Midwest. All right? *Michigan* is the Midwest, God knows why. This is the

Plains: a state of mind, right, some spiritual affliction, like the Blues.

BILL: "Are you okay?" "I'm fine. Just got the Plains."

(They laugh. He reaches up and touches her neck tenderly.)

BARBARA: Don't.

(She pulls away. They look away from one another, an uncomfortable moment.)

(Regarding Jean) What, is she smoking a fucking cigar?

BILL: She's coming.

(Jean arrives on the front porch, carrying a suitcase.)

You ready, kiddo?

JEAN: Yeah, sure.

BARBARA: All right. *(Gives Jean a quick kiss)* You're precious. I'm having a hot flash. All right . . . here goes.

(Lights up on the entryway as Barbara, Bill and Jean enter.)

Mom?!

(Lights up on the dining room. Mattie Fae and Charlie travel from the dining room to the entryway. The following salutations are quick and overlapping, and they range from forte [Mattie Fae] to piano [Ivy].)

MATTIE FAE: Oh my God, Barbara!—   BARBARA: Hi, Aunt Mattie Fae—

MATTIE FAE: You give me some sugar!

(Barbara and Mattie Fae hug.)

(Over Barbara's shoulder) Hi, Bill! Look how skinny you are!
BILL: Hi, Mattie Fae.
MATTIE FAE: Oh my gosh, will you look at this one? Come here and give your Aunt Mattie Fae some sugar!

(Mattie Fae and Jean hug. Bill and Charlie shake hands.)

BILL: Hi, Charlie.
CHARLIE: 'Lo, Bill. Man, you have dropped some weight, haven't you?
MATTIE FAE *(Still to Jean)*: My gosh, you're so big! And look at your big boobs! They're so big! Last time I saw you, you looked just like a little boy!

(Barbara and Charlie hug.)

CHARLIE: Hello, sweetheart.
BARBARA: Good to see you, Uncle Charlie.
CHARLIE: You too.
MATTIE FAE: Oh, I can't get over that one, she's just too much. Come here, Bill, and give me some sugar!

(Charlie mushes Jean's shoulder, kisses her on the temple.)

CHARLIE: Lovely to see you, dear.
JEAN: Yeah, same here.
CHARLIE *(Gently mocking)*: Same here, same here.

(Violet appears on the stairway, followed by Ivy. Violet bursts into tears, rushes to Barbara, clenches her. Ivy watches from the stairs.)

BARBARA: It's okay, Mom. I'm here, I'm here.

(Violet weeps. The others are awkwardly respectful of the moment.)

Shhh, it's okay, I'm here.

BILL *(To Charlie)*: No word then?

CHARLIE: No.   MATTIE FAE: No, huh-uh.

BARBARA: It's okay, Mom.

VIOLET: What am I going to do? What am I going to do?

BARBARA: Well, we can talk about that. Did you see Bill and Jean?

(Violet takes them in, disoriented.)

VIOLET: Yes. Hi, Bill.

BILL: Hello, Violet.

(Violet and Bill kiss.)

I'm sorry you're going through this.

(Violet holds Bill, cries.)

VIOLET: I'm just so scared.

(Mattie Fae reaches out, strokes Violet's back.)

MATTIE FAE: Of course you are, poor thing.

VIOLET: You're too thin.

BILL: Hardly.

VIOLET: Yes, you are.

(Violet sees Jean.)

Well, look at you.

MATTIE FAE: I know, isn't she something else? Look at her boobs!

JEAN: O-kay, we've all stared at my tits now.

MATTIE FAE: They're just so darn big.

CHARLIE: Mattie Fae . . .

(Violet hugs Jean.)

VIOLET: You're just the prettiest thing. Thank you for coming to see me.

JEAN: No problem.

BARBARA: Ivy, I didn't see you up there.

IVY *(Descending the stairs)*: It looked crowded.

BARBARA: God, you look good. Doesn't she look good, Bill?

BILL: Yes, she does.

BARBARA: I love your hair, that looks great.

VIOLET: She had it straightened.

BARBARA: I know, it looks great.

(Ivy and Jean wave.)

IVY: Hi, Jean.

JEAN: Hi.

(Violet pulls Barbara into the living room. The others follow.)

VIOLET: Barbara, or Bill, it doesn't matter, I need you to go through Beverly's things and help me with some of this paperwork.

BARBARA: Well . . . we can   IVY: I was going to help
do that, Mom, we're here   with that—
for a while.

VIOLET: No, now that desk of his is such a mess and I get confused—

33

BILL: I'll take care of it, Violet—

BARBARA *(To Charlie)*: Which room are you in?

MATTIE FAE: We're headed back tonight.

VIOLET: You're going back?

MATTIE FAE: We have to, Vi, we left in such a rush we didn't get anyone to take care of those damn dogs.

VIOLET: You want to drive that hour and a half tonight?

MATTIE FAE: Not the way Charlie drives. Anyway, I know you want to spend some time with these girls.

VIOLET: Can't you call someone about the dogs? Or how about Little Charles, can't he take care of them?

CHARLIE: Well, yeah, I guess he could—

MATTIE FAE: No, he can't, either. We have to get back.

CHARLIE: Maybe we should call him, Mattie Fae—

MATTIE FAE: We talked about this.

CHARLIE: I know, but—

MATTIE FAE *(To Violet)*: You've got all these people here and not enough beds—

VIOLET: You can stay at Ivy's place.

IVY *(Beat)*: Yeah, sure. I've got room.

MATTIE FAE *(To Charlie)*: We talked about this.

BARBARA: You all can figure that out on your own. So, Mom? Jean can stay in the attic?

VIOLET: No, that's where what's-her-name lives.

IVY: Johnna.

BARBARA: Who's Johnna?

VIOLET: She's the Indian who lives in my attic.

BARBARA: She's the what?

(Johnna enters.)

JOHNNA: Hi, I'm Johnna. Welcome home.

SCENE 2

Barbara, Bill and Violet are in the dining room with coffee and pie. Violet's pills are starting to kick in.

Elsewhere in the house: Johnna reads a book in her attic bedroom; Jean listens to an iPod on the second-floor landing.

VIOLET: Saturday. Saturday morning. That girl, the Indian girl made us biscuits and gravy. We ate some, we . . . he walked out the door, that door right there. And that was it.

BARBARA: That was the last time you saw him.

VIOLET: I went to bed Saturday night and got up Sunday morning . . . still no Beverly. I didn't make much of it, thought he'd gone out on a bender.

BARBARA: Why would he do that? Not like he couldn't drink at home. Unless you were riding his ass.

VIOLET: I never said anything to him about his drinking, never got on him about it.

BARBARA: Really.

VIOLET: Barbara, I swear. He could drink himself into obliv-uh, obliv-en-em . . .

BARBARA: Oblivion.

BILL: So Sunday, still no sign of him . . .

VIOLET: Yes, Sunday, no sign. I started getting worried, don'tcha know, and that's when I got so worked up about that safety deposit box. We kept an awful lot of cash in that box, some jewelry, expensive jewelry. I had a diamond ring in that box appraised at over seven thousand dollars—

BARBARA: Wait, wait, wait, I'm missing something, why do you care about the safety deposit box?

VIOLET: Well, I know what you'll say about this, but. Your father and I had a urge-ment—arrangement. If something were to ever happen to one of us, the other one would go empty that safety deposit box.

BARBARA: *Because . . .*

BILL: It gets rolled into the estate, then goes to *probate.*

VIOLET: Right, that's right—

BARBARA: You're such a fucking cynic.

VIOLET: I knew you would *disapprove*—

BARBARA *(Impatient)*: Okay, fine, so what about the safety deposit box?—

VIOLET: I had to wait for the bank to open on Monday. And after I emptied that box, I called the police and reported him missing. Monday morning.

BARBARA: And you're just now calling me, today, on *Thursday.*

VIOLET: *I* didn't call you.

BARBARA: You had Ivy call me. *Five days later.*

VIOLET: I didn't want to worry you, honey—

BARBARA: *Jesus Christ.*

BILL: Vi, you sure there wasn't some event that triggered his leaving, some incident?

VIOLET: You mean like a fight.

BILL: Yes.

VIOLET: No. And we fought enough . . . *you* know . . . but no, he just left.

BARBARA: Maybe he just needed some time away from you.

VIOLET: That's nice of you to say.

BARBARA: Hey, that's no crime. Being married is hard.

BILL: Under the best of circumstances.

BARBARA: But nothing. Not, "See you later," or "I'm taking a walk."

(Violet shakes her head.)

Good old unfathomable Dad.

VIOLET: Oh. That man. What I first fell of with—fell in love with, you know, was his mystery. I thought it was sexy as hell. You knew he was the smartest one in the room, knew if he'd just say something . . . knock you out. But he'd just stand there, little smile on his face . . . not say a word. Sexy.

BARBARA: Yeah, that "mystery" can cut both ways.

BILL: And you can't think of anything different or unusual, or—

VIOLET: He hired this woman. He didn't ask me, just hired this woman to come here and live in our house. Few days before he left.

BARBARA: You don't want her here.

VIOLET: I don't know what she's doing here. She's stranger in my house. There's an *Indian* in my house.

BILL *(Laughing)*: You have some problem with Indians, Violet?

VIOLET: I don't know what to say to an Indian.

BARBARA: They're called Native Americans now, Mom.

VIOLET: *Who* calls them that? Who *makes* that decision?

BARBARA: It's what they like to be called.

VIOLET: They aren't any more native than me.

BARBARA: In fact, they are.

VIOLET: What's wrong with "Indian"?

BARBARA: Why is it so hard to just call people what they want?—

VIOLET: Let's just call the dinosaurs "Native Americans" while we're at it.

BARBARA: She may be an Indian, but she makes the best goddamn apple pie I ever ate in my life.

BILL: It is good, isn't it?

BARBARA: Oh, man—

VIOLET: A cook? So he hired a cook? It doesn't make any sense. We don't eat.

BARBARA: That sounds healthy.

VIOLET: We eat, cheese and saltines, or a ham sandwich. But I can't tell you the last time that stove, oh . . . turned on. Years.

BARBARA: And now you get biscuits and gravy. Kind of nice, huh?

VIOLET: Nice for you, now. But you'll be gone soon enough, never to return.

BARBARA *(A warning)*: Mom.

VIOLET: When was the last time you were here?

BARBARA: Don't get started on that—

VIOLET: Really, I don't even remember.

BARBARA: I'm very dutiful, Mom, I call, I write, I send presents—

VIOLET: You do not *write*—

BARBARA: I send presents on birthdays and Mother's Day—

VIOLET: Because you're "dutiful."

BARBARA: Don't you quote me.

BILL: All right, now—

VIOLET: You're grown-up people, growed-ups. You go where you want—

BARBARA: I have a lot of obligations, I have a daughter starting high school in a couple of—

VIOLET: That right? Last time I saw her she's grade school—

BARBARA: I won't talk about this—

VIOLET: I don't care about you two, really. I'd just like to see my granddaughter every now and again.

BARBARA: Well, you're seeing her now.

VIOLET: But your father. You broke his heart when you moved away.

BARBARA: That is wildly unfair.

BILL: Am I going to have to separate you two?

VIOLET: You know you were Beverly's favorite; don't pretend you don't know that.

BARBARA: I don't *want* to know that. I'd prefer to think my parents loved all their children equally.

VIOLET: I'm sure you'd prefer to think that Santy Claus brought you presents at Christmas, too, but it just isn't so. If you'd had more than one child, you'd realize a parent always has favorites. Mattie Fae was my mother's favorite. Big deal. I got used to it. You were your daddy's favorite.

BARBARA: Great. Thanks.

(*Pause.*)

VIOLET: Broke his heart.

BARBARA: What was I supposed to do?! Colorado offered Bill twice the money he was making at TU—

BILL: Why are you even getting into this?

38

BARBARA: —and they were willing to hire me, too. Daddy knew we had to take those jobs. You think he wouldn't have jumped at the chance Bill got?

VIOLET: Now you're wrong there. You never would've gotten Beverly Weston out of Oklahoma. And don't think he didn't have his opportunities, either, after *Meadowlark* came out.

BILL: I'm sure.

VIOLET: After *Meadowlark* was published, he got offers from everywhere in the country, lots better places than Colorado.

BARBARA: Now you want to knock Colorado.

VIOLET: It's not hard to do.

BILL: Barbara, Jesus—

BARBARA: Daddy's book came out forty years ago. Academia's very different now, it's extremely competitive.

VIOLET: Please, tell me all about *academia*.

BARBARA: Daddy gave me his blessing, and I didn't even ask for it.

VIOLET: 'Swhat he told *you*.

BARBARA: Now you're going to tell me the *true* story, some terrible shit Daddy said behind my back?

BILL: Hey, enough. Everybody's a little on edge—

VIOLET: Beverly didn't say terrible things behind your back—

BILL: Vi, come on—

VIOLET: He just told me he's disappointed in you because you settled.

BARBARA: Is that supposed to be a comment on Bill? Daddy never said anything like that to you—

VIOLET: Your father thought you had talent, as a writer.

BARBARA: If he thought that, and I doubt he did, he was wrong. Anyway, what difference does it make? It's my life. I can do what I want. So he was disappointed in me because I settled for a beautiful family and a teaching career, is that what you're saying? What a load of absolute horseshit.

VIOLET: Oh, horseshit, horseshit, let's all say horseshit. Say horseshit, Bill.

BILL: Horseshit.

(Bill exits to the kitchen.)

BARBARA: Are you high?

VIOLET: No.

BARBARA: No, are you high? I mean literally. Are you taking something?

VIOLET: A muscle relaxer.

BARBARA: Listen to me: I will not go through this with you again.

VIOLET: Go through what?

BARBARA: These fucking pills.

VIOLET: They're muscle relaxers—

BARBARA: I will not do this again.

VIOLET: I don't know what you're talking about.

BARBARA: The psych ward? Calls at three A.M. about people in your backyard?

VIOLET: You're so much drama—

BARBARA: The police, all the rest of it? You *do* know what I'm talking about. You spent a goddamn fortune on these fucking pills—

VIOLET: Stop yelling at me!

BARBARA: —and then you spent another fortune getting off them.

VIOLET: It's not the same thing, I didn't have a reason.

BARBARA: So now it's okay to get hooked because you have a reason.

VIOLET: I'm not hooked on anything.

BARBARA: I don't know if you are or not, I'm just saying I won't go—

VIOLET: I'm not. I'm in pain.

BARBARA: Because of your mouth.

VIOLET: Yes, because my mouth burns from the chemo-theeeahh.

BARBARA: Are you in a lot of pain?

VIOLET *(Starting to cry)*: Yes, I'm in pain. I have got . . . gotten cancer. In my mouth. And it burns like a . . . bullshit. And Beverly's disappeared and you're yelling at me.

BARBARA: I'm not yelling at you.

(Bill returns.)

VIOLET: You couldn't come home when I got cancer but as soon as Beverly disappeared you rushed back—
BARBARA: I'm sorry, I . . . you're right. I'm sorry.

(Violet cries. Barbara kneels in front of her, takes her hand.)

You know where I think he is? I think he got some whiskey . . . a carton of cigarettes, couple of good spy novels . . . aannnd I think he got out on the boat, steered it to a nice spot, somewhere in the shade, close to shore . . . and he's fishing, and reading, and drinking, and if the mood strikes him, maybe even writing a little. I think he's safe. And I think he'll walk through that door . . . any time.

(Lights down on the dining room, and up on the attic, where Johnna is reading. Jean has put away her iPod and now ascends the stairs.)

JEAN: Hi.
JOHNNA: Hello.
JEAN: Am I bugging you?
JOHNNA: No, do you need something?
JEAN: No, I thought maybe you'd like to smoke a bowl with me?
JOHNNA: No, thank you.
JEAN: Okay. I didn't know.

(Jean stands, looking at her.)

Am I bugging you?
JOHNNA: No, huh-uh.
JEAN: Okay. Do you mind if I smoke a bowl?
JOHNNA: I. No, I—

JEAN: 'Cause there's no place I can go. Y'know, I'm staying right by Grandma's room, and if I go outside, they're gonna wonder—

JOHNNA: Right—

JEAN: Mom and Dad don't mind. You won't get into trouble or anything.

JOHNNA: Okay.

JEAN: Okay. You sure?

(Johnna nods. From her pocket, Jean takes a small glass pipe and a clear cigarette wrapper holding a bud of marijuana. She fixes the pipe.)

I say they don't mind. If they knew I stuck this bud under the cap of Dad's deodorant before our flight and then sat there sweating like in that movie *Maria Full of Grace.* Did you see that?

JOHNNA: I don't think so.

JEAN: I just mean they don't mind that I smoke pot. Dad doesn't. Mom kind of does. She thinks it's bad for me. I think the real reason it bugs her is 'cause Dad smokes pot, too, and she wishes he didn't. Dad's much cooler than Mom, really. Well, that's not true. He's just cooler in that way, I guess.

(Jean smokes. She offers the smoldering pipe to Johnna.)

(Holding her breath) You sure?

JOHNNA: Yes. No. I'm fine.

JEAN: No, he's really not cooler. *(Exhales smoke)* He and Mom are separated right now.

JOHNNA: I'm sorry.

JEAN: He's fucking one of his students which is pretty uncool, if you ask me. Some people would think that's cool, like those dicks who teach with him in the Humanities Department because they're all fucking their students or wish they were fucking their students. "Lo-liii-ta." I mean,

I don't care and all, he can fuck whoever he wants and he's a teacher and that's who teachers meet, students. He was just a turd the way he went about it and didn't give Mom a chance to respond or anything. What sucks now is that Mom's watching me like a hawk, like, she's afraid I'll have some post-divorce freak-out and become some heroin addict or shoot everybody at school. Or God forbid, lose my virginity. I don't know what it is about Dad splitting that put Mom on hymen patrol. Do you have a boyfriend?

JOHNNA: No, not these days.

JEAN: Me neither. I did go with this boy Josh for like almost a year but he was retarded. Are your parents still together?

JOHNNA: They passed away.

JEAN: Oh. I'm sorry.

JOHNNA: That's okay. Thank you.

JEAN: Oh, fuck, no, I'm really sorry, I feel fucking terrible now.

JOHNNA: It's okay.

JEAN: Oh God. Okay. Were you close with them?

JOHNNA: Yeah.

JEAN: Okay, another stupid question there, Jean, real good. Wow. Like: "Are you close to your parents?"

JOHNNA: Not everybody is.

JEAN: Yeah, right? So that's what I meant. Thanks.

(Johnna takes a framed photograph from her nightstand and hands it to Jean.)

Oh, wow. This is them.

JOHNNA: Mm-hm, their wedding picture.

JEAN: That's sweet. Their costumes are fantastic.

(Johnna smiles. Jean hands the photograph back, walks around the room.)

This is a great room. Very *Night of the Hunter.* This used to be my room when we'd come and stay.

JOHNNA: I'm sorry.

JEAN: Oh. No, I . . . it doesn't matter to me. It's just a room. *(Beat)* What are you reading?

JOHNNA: T. S. Eliot.

JEAN: That's cool.

JOHNNA: Your grandfather loaned it to me.

JEAN: Grandpa's weird. Mom freaked when she got the call from Aunt Ivy this morning, just like . . . freaked. I've never seen her like that. I couldn't get her to calm down. It was weird. I guess it's not weird that she freaked out, but like, to see your mom freak like that, like you've never seen before, y'know? And we're real close. Did you ever see your parents freak out?

JOHNNA: They weren't really the type.

JEAN: Yeah, right? So like imagine if you did just one day see them like totally lose their shit, just like, "Whoa."

(Jean reaches, touches a beaded pouch in the shape of a turtle hanging from Johnna's neck.)

I like your necklace.

JOHNNA: Thank you.

JEAN: Did you make that?

JOHNNA: My grandma.

JEAN: It's a turtle, right?

JOHNNA: Mm-hm.

JEAN: It feels like there's something in it.

JOHNNA: My umbilical cord.

(Jean recoils, wipes her hand on her pant's leg. Johnna laughs.)

JEAN: Ewww, are you serious?

JOHNNA: Yes.

JEAN: Oh my God. That's kind of gross.

JOHNNA: It's not unsanitary.

JEAN: Why would you do that, is it some kind of . . . ?

JOHNNA: It's a Cheyenne tradition.

JEAN: You're Cheyenne.

JOHNNA: Mm-hm.

JEAN: Like that movie *Powwow Highway*. Did you see that?

JOHNNA: When a Cheyenne baby is born, their umbilical cord is dried and sewn into this pouch. Turtles for girls, lizards for boys. And we wear it for the rest of our lives.

JEAN: Wow.

JOHNNA: Because if we lose it, our souls belong nowhere and after we die our souls will walk the Earth looking for where we belong.

JEAN: Don't say anything about Mom and Dad splitting up, okay? They're trying to play this kind of low-key.

SCENE 3

Barbara unfolds the hide-a-bed in the living room. Bill enters from the study, carrying a thin hardback book.

BILL: Look what I found. Isn't that great?

BARBARA: We have copies.

BILL: I don't think I remember a hardback edition. I forgot there was ever a time they published poetry in hardback. Hell, I forgot there was ever a time they published poetry at all.

BARBARA: I'm not going to be able to sleep in this heat.

BILL: I wonder if this is worth something.

BARBARA: I'm sure it's not.

BILL: You never know. First edition, hardback, mint condition? Academy Fellowship, uh . . . Wallace Stevens Award? That's right, isn't it?

BARBARA: Mm-hm.

BILL: This book was a big deal.

BARBARA: It wasn't that big a deal.

BILL: In those circles, it was.

BARBARA: Those are small circles.

BILL *(Reads from the book)*: "Dedicated to my Violet." That's nice. Christ . . . I can't imagine the kind of pressure he must've felt after this came out. Probably every word he wrote after this, he had to be thinking, "What are they going to say about this? Are they going to compare it to *Meadowlark?*"

BARBARA: Did Jean go to bed?

BILL: She just turned out the light. You would think, though, at some point, you just say, "To hell with this," and you write something anyway and who cares what they say about it. I mean I don't know, myself—

BARBARA: Will you please shut up about that fucking book?!

BILL: What's the matter?

BARBARA: You are just dripping with envy over these . . . thirty poems my father wrote back in the fucking sixties, for God's sake. Don't you hear yourself?

BILL: You're mistaken. I have great admiration for these poems, not envy—

BARBARA: Reciting his list of awards—

BILL: I was merely talking about the value—

BARBARA: My father didn't write anymore for a lot of reasons, but critical opinion was not one of them, hard as that may be for you to believe. I know how important that stuff is to you.

BILL: What are you attacking me for? I haven't done anything.

BARBARA: I'm sure that's what you tell *Sissy*, too, so she can comfort you, reassure you: "No, Billy, you haven't done anything."

BILL: What does that have to do—why are you bringing that up?

BARBARA: They're all symptoms of your male menopause, whether it's you struggling with the "creative question," or screwing a girl who still wears a retainer.

BILL: All right, look. I'm here for you. Because I want to be with you, in a difficult time. But I'm not going to be held hostage in this room so you can attack me—

BARBARA: I'm sorry, I didn't mean to hold you hostage. You really should go then.

BILL: I'm not going anywhere. I flew to Oklahoma to be here with you and now you're stuck with me. And her name is Cindy.

BARBARA: I know her stupid name. At least do me the courtesy of recognizing when I'm demeaning you.

BILL: Violet really has a way of putting you in attack mode, you know it?

BARBARA: She doesn't have anything to do with it.

BILL: Don't you believe it. You feel such rage for her that you can't help dishing it my direction—

BARBARA: I swear to God, you psychoanalyze me right now, I skin you.

BILL: You may not agree with my methods, but you know I'm right.

BARBARA: Your "methods." Thank you, Doctor, but I actually don't need any help from my mother to feel rage.

BILL: You want to argue? Is that what you need to do? Well, pick a subject, all right, and let me know what it is, so I can have a fighting chance—

BARBARA: The subject is me! I am the subject, you narcissistic motherfucker! I am in pain! I need help!

(Jean enters from the second-floor hallway, sits on the stairway, listens.)

BILL: I've copped to being a narcissist. We're the products of a narcissistic generation.

BARBARA: You can't do it, can you? You can't talk about me for two seconds—

BILL: You called me a narcissist! And when I try to talk about you, you accuse me of psychoanalyzing you—!

BARBARA: You do understand that it hurts, to go from sharing a bed with you for twenty-three years to sleeping by myself.

BILL: I'm here, now.

BARBARA: Men always say shit like that, as if the past and the future don't exist.

BILL: Can we not make this a gender discussion?

BARBARA: Do men really believe that here and now is enough? It's just horseshit, to avoid talking about the things they're afraid to say.

BILL: I'm not necessarily keen on the notion of saying things that would hurt you.

BARBARA: Like what?

BILL: Don't.

BARBARA: What? Say it. You must realize there's nothing you can say that would hurt me any more than I'm already hurting. The damage is done.

BILL: I think you're wrong. I think you get in this masochistic frame of mind that actually desires to be hurt more than—

BARBARA: *What?!*

BILL: Barbara, please, we have enough on our hands with your parents right now. Let's not revisit all this.

BARBARA: *R*evisit, when did we visit this to begin with? You pulled the rug out from under me. I still don't know what happened. Do I bore you, intimidate you, disgust you? Is this just about the pleasures of young flesh, teenage pussy? I really need to know.

BILL: You need to know *now?* You want to have this discussion with Beverly missing, and your mother as crazy as a loon, and our daughter twenty feet away? Do you really want to do this now?

BARBARA: No. You're right. I'll just hunker down for a cozy night's sleep. Next to my husband.

(She calmly gets under the covers.)

BILL: This discussion deserves our care. And patience. We'll both be in a better frame of mind to talk about this once your father's come home.

BARBARA: My father's dead, Bill.

(She rolls onto her side, her back to Bill.)

48

SCENE 4

Red and blue police flashers bounce across the exterior of the house. Sheriff Gilbeau stands on the front porch. The rest of the house is dark.

Johnna, wearing a robe, quietly knocks on the stereo cabinet in the living room.

BARBARA: Mm . . . what?
JOHNNA: Excuse me . . . it's Johnna.
BARBARA: What?
JOHNNA: Excuse me—
BARBARA: What is it?
JOHNNA: The sheriff's here.
BILL: Turn on the light.

(Johnna turns on a lamp, temporarily blinding Bill and Barbara.)

JOHNNA: The sheriff is here.

(Pause. This sinks in. Then Bill and Barbara scramble out of bed.)

Should I wake Mrs. Weston?
BARBARA: I don't know. Bill?
BILL: Yeah, you better get her up.

(Johnna leaves the room. Jean enters the second-floor landing, bleary-eyed, as Bill and Barbara scurry into clothes. Barbara climbs the stairs.)

JEAN: What's going on?
BARBARA: The sheriff is here.
JEAN: What?
BARBARA: Go back to bed, honey.
JEAN: Why are the police here?

BARBARA: I don't know, sweetheart, please go back to bed.

(Offstage, an attempt to alert Violet. Johnna knocks on Violet's bedroom door.)

JOHNNA: Mrs. Weston? *(Knocks again)* Mrs. Weston.

(Barbara knocks loudly.)

BARBARA: Mom? . . . Mom, wake up.
VIOLET: Huh?
BARBARA: Wake up, the sheriff's here.
VIOLET: Did you call them?
BARBARA: No.
VIOLET: I dig in call them.
BARBARA: Mom. The sheriff is here. You need to wake up and come downstairs.
VIOLET: Inna esther?
BARBARA: What?
VIOLET: Inna esther broke. 'N' pays me 'em . . . sturck . . . struck.
BILL *(From the bottom of the stairs)*: Come on.
BARBARA *(To Bill)*: What . . . ?
BILL: Come on. Leave her there.

(Barbara halfway descends the stairs, trailed by Johnna, as Bill admits Sheriff Gilbeau, shakes hands.)

Bill Fordham, Barbara's husband.
SHERIFF GILBEAU: Hello. Hi, Barbara.
BARBARA: Oh my God, I know you. Oh my God, Deon . . .
SHERIFF GILBEAU: Yes, ma'am. I'm afraid I have some bad news for you folks.
BARBARA: Okay—
SHERIFF GILBEAU: We found your father. He's dead.
BILL: Oh dear God.

(Barbara keens immediately, sinks to her knees on the stairway. Johnna wraps one hand around Barbara's middle, places the other hand firmly on Barbara's forehead. Jean sits down on a step.)

SHERIFF GILBEAU: I am sorry.

BILL: What happened?

SHERIFF GILBEAU: We got a call from the lake patrol a few hours ago that Mr. Weston's boat was found washed up on a sandbar. We were planning to drag the lake this morning around that area, southeast, when we got another call. Couple old boys running jug lines in the cove, uh . . . hooked . . . Mr. Weston. And pulled him up.

BILL: Now? This time of night?

SHERIFF GILBEAU: These guys run those lines early.

BILL: He drowned. That's how he died, from drowning.

SHERIFF GILBEAU: Yes, sir.

BILL: Is there any possibility . . . *any* possibility that it's not him?

SHERIFF GILBEAU: Given the proximity of the boat to where the body was found, we're pretty sure it's Mr. Weston.

(Barbara suddenly dries her eyes, shrugs Johnna's grasp, stands.)

BARBARA: All right. Okay. So what happens? What do we do now?

SHERIFF GILBEAU: I need a relative to come with me to positively identify the body.

BILL: To your station house.

SHERIFF GILBEAU: No, sir, he's still at the lake.

BARBARA: Oh God, I don't think I can do this.

SHERIFF GILBEAU: I'm sorry.

BILL: I'll go. Can I go? Can I do it?

SHERIFF GILBEAU: I need a blood relative. But if Barbara is the one to identify him, I suggest you come along.

BARBARA: Bill, I can't do it.

BILL: Honey, what choice do we have?

JEAN: I can do it. I'm a blood relative.

BARBARA: No, no. No, I'll do it. I will.

(Johnna exits to the kitchen, turns on the lights, starts a pot of coffee.)

BILL: Can we have a couple of minutes to get ready?

SHERIFF GILBEAU: Yes, sir. Barbara?

(She turns to him.)

I'm very sorry. This is the hardest part of my job. And I'm . . . to do it for someone you know . . . I'm just . . . very sorry.

(She nods.)

BILL: What do you want to do about your mother?

BARBARA: I . . . I . . . fuck it. *(Laughs)* Fuck it. I'll go . . . put some clothes on.

BILL: I'll be right up. Jean, help your mother, okay?

(Barbara and Jean exit down the second-floor hallway. Bill pulls Sheriff Gilbeau into the study.)

Is there any way to determine if he—I mean, is this an accident, or suicide?—

SHERIFF GILBEAU: There's really no way to tell.

BILL: What do you think happened? I mean . . . what's your guess?

SHERIFF GILBEAU: Suicide. I would guess suicide. But the official cause of death is "drowning." And that's the extent of it.

BILL: I understand.

SHERIFF GILBEAU: I should warn you. That body has been in the water for all of three days.

BILL: Right.

SHERIFF GILBEAU: I think you should try to prepare your wife, if you can.

BILL: "Prepare her . . ."

SHERIFF GILBEAU: What happens to a body. It's very bloated. It's an ugly color. And fish have eaten the eyes.

BILL: Oh Christ. How does a person jump in the water . . . and choose not to swim?

SHERIFF GILBEAU: I don't think you do unless you really mean business.

BILL: Choose not to swim.

(Lights shift to the second-floor landing as Barbara and Jean enter. Jean sits on the window seat as Barbara rakes a brush through her hair.)

JEAN: What about Aunt Ivy?

BARBARA: I guess we'll stop there on the way back and tell her. Christ, I need to call Karen, too. What the fuck am I brushing my hair for?

(She throws the brush. She slumps on the window seat next to Jean.)

I used to go out with that boy. With that man.

JEAN: What man?

BARBARA: The sheriff.

JEAN: You did?

BARBARA: Yeah, in high school. He was my prom date.

JEAN: You're kidding.

BARBARA: The day of the prom, his father got drunk and stole his car. Stole his own son's car and went somewhere. Mexico. Deon showed up at the door, wearing this awful tuxedo. He'd been crying, I could tell. And he confessed he didn't have a way to take me to the prom. I just felt awful for him, so I told him we'd walk. About three miles. I busted a heel and we both got so sweaty and dirty. We gave up . . .

got a six-pack and broke into the chapel, stayed up all night talking and kissing. And now he's here telling me . . . oh, it's just surreal. Thank God we can't tell the future. We'd never get out of bed.

(She fixes Jean with a look.)

Listen to me: die after me, all right? I don't care what else you do, where you go, how you screw up your life, just . . . survive. Outlive me, please.

JEAN: I'll do my best.

(Bill enters.)

BILL: You ready?
BARBARA: Give me a second.

(Lights shift to the study, where Sheriff Gilbeau waits. Violet, wearing silk pajamas, shakily descends the stairs, crosses into the study.)

VIOLET: Izza story.
SHERIFF GILBEAU: Hello, Violet.
VIOLET: Barely's back.
SHERIFF GILBEAU: I beg your pardon?
VIOLET: Did sum Beer-ley come home?
SHERIFF GILBEAU: Ma'am.

(Violet shuffles up to Sheriff Gilbeau.)

VIOLET: Gizza cig . . . some cigezze? Cig-zezz, cig-zizz, cig-uhzzz.

(She laughs at her own inability to speak. Sheriff Gilbeau takes a Pall Mall from his shirt pocket, hands it to her. She stands, sways, holding the cigarette in her mouth. He lights it.)

In the archa, archa-tex? I'm in the bottom. Izza bottom of them. Inna . . . ell.

(She shuffles to the stereo in the living room . . .)

His master's voice.

(. . . and plays a song: "Lay Down, Sally," by Clapton. Sheriff Gilbeau trails her into the living room.)

Mm, good beat. Right?

SHERIFF GILBEAU: Yes, ma'am.

(She does a jerky little dance, puffing on her cigarette.)

VIOLET: Barbara?! Is Barbara here?!

SHERIFF GILBEAU: She's upstairs.

VIOLET: Barbara?! Izza time in duhh . . . izza time? What's time?!

SHERIFF GILBEAU: It's about 5:45.

VIOLET: BARB'RA! BARB'RA!

(Barbara, Bill, Jean and Johnna enter from various points in the house. Violet sees them, continues her tight little dance.)

Idn't it's good beat? Inna good beats. Mmm, I been on the music . . . pell-man onna sheriff. C. J.'s boy. Right? Donna two inna school? Armen in tandel s'lossle, s'lost? Lost?! From the day, the days. Am Beerly . . . and Beverly lost?

(Violet abandons her dance, separates invisible threads in the air. The others stand frozen, staring at her.)

And then you're here. And Barbara, and then you're here, and Beverly, and then you're here, and then you're here, and then you're here, and then you're here, and then you're

55

here, and then you're here, and then you're here, and then you're here, and then you're here, and then you're here, and then you're here, and then you're here, and then you're here, and then you're here, and then you're here, and then you're here . . .

(Blackout.)

ACT TWO

The house has been manifestly refreshed, presumably by Johnna's hand. The dull, dusty finish has been replaced by the transparent gleam of function.

Of note:

The study has been reorganized. Stacks of paper are neater, books are shelved. The dining room table is set with the fine china, candles, a floral centerpiece. In a corner of the dining room, a "kid's table," with seating for two, is also set. The warm, clean kitchen now bubbles and steams, redolent of collard and kale.

At rise:

Three o'clock of an eternal Oklahoma afternoon. The body of Beverly Weston has just been buried.

Violet, relatively sober now, in a handsome modern black dress, stands in Beverly's study, a bottle of pills in her hand.

Elsewhere in the house: Karen and Barbara are in the dining room. Johnna is in the kitchen.

VIOLET: August . . . your month. Locusts are raging. "Summer psalm become summer wrath." 'Course it's only August out there. In *here* . . . who knows?

All right . . . okay. "The Carriage held but just Ourselves," dum-de-dum . . . mm, best I got . . . Emily Dickinson's all I got . . . something something, "Horse's Heads Were Toward Eternity . . ."

(She takes a pill.)

That's for me . . . one for me . . .

(She picks up the hardback copy of Meadowlark, *flips to the dedication.)*

"Dedicated to my Violet." Put that one in marble.

(She drops the book on the desk. She takes a pill.)

For the girls, God love 'em. That's all I can dedicate to you, sorry to say. Other than them . . . not one thing. No thing. You think I'll weep for you? Think I'll play that part, like we played the others?

(She takes a pill.)

You made your choice. You made this happen. *You* answer for this . . . not me. Not me. This is not mine.

(Lights crossfade to the dining room. Barbara and Karen, wearing black dresses, fold napkins, munch food from a relish tray, etc.)

KAREN: The present. Today, here and now. I think I spent so much of my early life thinking about what's to come, y'know, who would I marry, would he be a lawyer or a football player, would he be dark-haired and good-looking and broad-shouldered. I spent a lot of time in that bedroom upstairs pretending my pillow was my husband and I'd ask him about his day at work and what was happening at the office, and did he like the dinner I made for him and where were we going to vacation that winter and he'd surprise me with tickets to Belize and we'd kiss—I mean I'd kiss my pillow, make out with my pillow, and then I'd tell him I'd been to the doctor that day and I'd found out I was pregnant. I know how pathetic all that sounds now, but it was innocent enough . . .

Then real life takes over because it always does—

BARBARA: —uh-huh—

KAREN: —and things work out differently than you'd planned. That pillow was a better husband than any real man I'd ever met; this parade of men fails to live up to your expectations, all of them so much less than Daddy or Bill (you know I always envied you finding Bill). And you punish yourself, tell yourself it's your fault you can't find a good one, you've only deluded yourself into thinking they're better than they are. I don't know how well you remember Andrew . . .

BARBARA: No, I remember.

KAREN: That's the best example: here's a guy I loved so intensely, and all the things he did wrong were just opportunities for me to make things right. So if he cheated on me or he called me a cunt, I'd think to myself, "No, you love him, you love him forever, and here's an opportunity to make an adjustment in the way you view the world." And I can't say when the precise moment was that I looked in the mirror and said, "Okay, moron," and walked out, but it kicked off this whole period of reflection, just swamped in this sticky recollection. How had I screwed it up, where'd I go wrong, and before you know it you can't move forward, you're just suspended there, you can't move forward because you can't stop thinking backward, I mean, you know . . . years! Years of punishment, self-loathing. And that's when I got into all those books and discussion groups—

BARBARA: And Scientology, too, right, or something like that?—

KAREN: Yes, exactly, and finally one day, I threw it all out, I just said, "No, it's *me*. It's just *me*, here and now, with my music on the stereo and my glass of wine and Bloomers my cat, and I don't need anything else, I can live my life with myself." And I got my license, threw myself into my work, sold a lot of houses, and that's when I met Steve. That's how it happens, of course, you only really find it when you're not looking for it, suddenly you turn around and there it is. And then the things you thought were so important aren't really important. I mean, when I made out with my pillow, I never imagined Steve! Here he is, you know, this kinda country club Chamber of Commerce guy, ten years older than me, but a thinker, you know, someone who's been around, and he's just so good. He's a good man and he's good to me and he's good *for* me.

BARBARA: That's great, Karen—

KAREN: He's got this great business and it's because he has these great ideas and he's unafraid to make his ideas realities, you know, he's not afraid of *doing*. I think men on the whole are better at that than women, don't you? *Doing*, just jumping in and *doing*, right or wrong, we'll figure out what it all means later. And the best thing about him, the best thing about him for me, is that now what I think about is *now*. I live *now*. My focus, my life, my world is *now*. I don't give a care about the past anymore, the mistakes I made, the way I *thought*, I won't go back there. And I've realized you can't plan the future, because as soon as you do, you know, something happens, some terrible thing happens—

BARBARA: Like your father drowning himself.

KAREN: Exactly! Exactly, that's exactly what I mean! That's not something you plan for! There's no contingency; you take it as it comes, here and now! Steve had a very important presentation today, for some bigwig government guys who could be very important for his business, something he's been putting together for months, and as soon as we heard about Daddy, he called and canceled his meeting. He has his priorities straight. And you know what the kicker is?

(Barbara waits.)

Do you know what the kicker is?
BARBARA: What's the kicker?
KAREN: We're going to Belize on our honeymoon.

(Johnna enters from the kitchen, bringing in a pitcher of iced tea.)

BARBARA: Sorry. Hot flash.
KAREN: I never told him my little Belize fantasy, he just up and surprised me with tickets for after the wedding.
BARBARA *(To Johnna)*: God, that smells good, what are we having?
JOHNNA: Um . . . baked chicken, fried potatoes, green bean casserole . . . some greens . . .
BARBARA: Did Mattie Fae bring her green bean casserole?
JOHNNA: Oh. I don't know. Should I not have made it?
BARBARA: No, it's good you did, hers is inedible.

(Johnna exits.)

KAREN: I mean, can you believe that about Belize?
BARBARA: That's terrific.
KAREN: I know you only just met him, but did you get a read off him? Did you like him?
BARBARA: We said two words to each other—

KAREN: But you still get a feel, don't you? Did you get a feel?

BARBARA: He seemed very nice, sweetheart—

KAREN: He *is*, and—

BARBARA: —but what I think about him doesn't matter. I'm not marrying him—

KAREN: You'll come to the wedding, won't you?

BARBARA: Yeah, when is it again?

KAREN: New Year's Day. One reason we chose New Year's is because I know you and Bill have a break from school and it's important to me that you're there.

BARBARA: It's in Sarasota?

KAREN: Miami. Didn't you know I moved to Miami?

BARBARA: Wait, yes, I did know that—

KAREN: That's where Steve's business—

BARBARA: —right, right.

KAREN: I guess what I'm telling you is that I'm finally happy. I've been really unhappy for most of my life, my adult life. I doubt you've been aware of that. I know our lives have led us apart, you, me and Ivy, and maybe we're not as close as we . . . as close as some families—

BARBARA: Yeah, we really need to talk about Mom, what to do about Mom—

KAREN: —but I think at least one reason for that is that I haven't wanted to live my unhappiness in full view of my family. But now I'm . . . well, I'm just really happy. And I'd really like us to maybe get to know each other a little better.

BARBARA: Yes. Yes.

(Karen wraps her arms around Barbara.)

Okay. Yes.

(They separate.)

Christ, where are they with the wine already?

KAREN: And see, there's another example, Steve doesn't know a soul here, but he jumped right in the car with Bill and Jean to go get the wine. He's family!

(Lights crossfade to the second-floor landing. Ivy enters, pursued by Violet, who carries a dress and a pair of high heels. Mattie Fae follows, rooting through a box of photographs.
Like Violet, Mattie Fae wears a black dress; Ivy wears a black suit. During the following, Barbara and Karen exit to the kitchen.)

IVY: I really don't want to.

VIOLET: It won't kill you to try it on—

MATTIE FAE *(Regarding photographs)*: Oh, this is a sweet one, Vi—

IVY: I find all this a tidge morbid, quite frankly—

MATTIE FAE: Look at this,   VIOLET: What's morbid
Ivy—   about it?

IVY: —and I'm really not prepared to look at these photographs right now—

VIOLET: This is a beautiful dress and it's very modern.

IVY: It's not my style, Mom—

MATTIE FAE: Where was this taken?—

VIOLET: You don't have a style, that's the whole point—

MATTIE FAE: Vi?

VIOLET *(Glancing at the photo)*: New York City. That's from the first book tour, New York—

IVY: You mean I don't have *your* style. I have a style of my own—

MATTIE FAE: "New York City, 1964"—

VIOLET: Honey, you wore a suit to your father's funeral. A woman doesn't wear a suit to a funeral—

IVY: God, you're weird; it's a black suit.

VIOLET: You look like a magician's assistant.

IVY: You know—

MATTIE FAE: Little Charles has been talking about moving to New York.

IVY: —why do you feel it necessary to—?   MATTIE FAE: Can you picture that?

VIOLET: Don't discourage him now—

MATTIE FAE: He wouldn't last a day in that city. They'd tear him apart.

IVY: Why do you feel it—?

MATTIE FAE: I could kill that kid—

IVY: Why do you feel it necessary to insult me?

VIOLET: Stop being so sensitive.

MATTIE FAE: He overslept? For my brother-in-law's funeral? A *noon* service?

IVY: I'm sure there's more to the story than—

MATTIE FAE: You shouldn't make excuses for him. That's what Charlie does, has always done. Just, "Oh, he overslept, la-di-da, I'll go pick him up at the bus station."

IVY: You're so hard on him.

MATTIE FAE: Boy's thirty-seven years old and *can't drive*?

VIOLET: He's a little different, I'll give you that.

IVY: I think you're being—

MATTIE FAE: Who *can't drive*?

IVY: I don't think you're very—

MATTIE FAE: I've seen a *chimp* drive.

VIOLET: Will you take off that cheap suit and try this on for me, please?

IVY: Cheap?! Did you call this—?!

MATTIE FAE: Is this the kind of thing you had in mind, Vi?

VIOLET: No, it's to go on the sideboard for the meal, so it should be something we easily recognize—

MATTIE FAE: You mean something big.

VIOLET: Yes. I have a frame we can—

IVY: This is the most expensive item of clothing I own.

VIOLET: I don't see what difference that makes, how much you paid for it. A suit of armor is expensive, too, but that doesn't make it appropriate—

MATTIE FAE: Well, *this* one's big, but it's of the *two* of you—

IVY: Why are you trying to give away your clothes?

MATTIE FAE: Do you mind if it's of the two of you?—

VIOLET: All this shit's going. I'm downgrading.

IVY: "Downgrading."

VIOLET: Down*sizing*, I'm downsizing.

IVY: You're "downsizing"—

MATTIE FAE: Vi, do you think this is—?

VIOLET: I'm serious, it's all going. I don't plan to spend the rest of my days walking around and looking at what used to be. I want that shit in the office gone, I want all these clothes I'm never going to wear gone, I want it all gone! I mean look at these fucking shoes. *(Holds up the high heels)* Can you picture me in these? Even if I didn't fall on my face, can you imagine anything less attractive, my swollen ankles and varicose veins? And my toenails, good God, anymore they could dig through cement.

(Mattie Fae holds a photograph in front of Violet.)

MATTIE FAE: Is this the idea?

VIOLET *(Takes the photograph)*: Look at me. *(Shows the photograph to Ivy)* Look at me.

IVY: You're beautiful, Mom.

VIOLET: I was beautiful. Not anymore.

MATTIE FAE: Oh, now—

IVY: You're still beautiful.

VIOLET: No. One of those lies we tell to give us comfort, but don't you believe it. Women are beautiful when they're young, and not after. Men can still preserve their sex appeal well into old age. I don't mean those men like you see with shorts and those little purses around their waists. Some men can maintain, if they embrace it . . . cragginess, weary masculinity. Women just get old and fat and wrinkly.

MATTIE FAE: I beg your pardon.

VIOLET: Think about what makes a young woman sexy. Think about the last time you went to the mall and saw some sweet little gal and thought, "She's a cute trick." What makes her that way? Taut skin, firm boobs, an ass above her knees—

MATTIE FAE: I'm still very sexy, thank you very much.

VIOLET: You're about as sexy as a wet cardboard box, Mattie Fae, you and me both. Don't kid yourself. Look . . . can we all just stop kidding ourselves? Wouldn't we be better off, all of us, if we stopped lying about these things and told the truth? "Women aren't sexy when they're old." I can live with that. Can you live with that?

MATTIE FAE: I can live with it, but I disagree. What about Sophia Loren? What about Lena Horne? She stayed sexy until she was eighty.

VIOLET: The world is round. Get over it. Now try this dress on.

IVY: I'm sorry, I won't.

VIOLET: Ivy.

IVY: All right, the heat in here is getting just stupid now—

VIOLET: Now listen to me: you don't know how to attract a man. I do. That's something I've always—

IVY: It's a funeral! We just buried my father, I'm not trying to attract—!

VIOLET: I'm not talking about today, dummy, this is something you can wear some—

IVY: I have a man. All right? I have a man.

(Mattie Fae turns her attention to Ivy.)

VIOLET: You said . . . you told me you weren't looking for a man—

IVY: And I'm not. Because I have one. Okay? Now will you leave it alone?

(Pause.)

VIOLET: No, I won't leave   MATTIE FAE: No, let's not leave
it alone.   it alone.

IVY: I wish you both could see the brainsick looks on your
    faces—
VIOLET: Who is it?
IVY: Nobody. Forget it—
VIOLET: No, no you don't, I want to know who you're—
IVY: I'm not talking about this—
MATTIE FAE: Ivy, please tell us—
IVY: No.
MATTIE FAE: Is he someone from school?
VIOLET: Tell me you're not back with Loser Barry.
IVY: No, it isn't Barry.
VIOLET: Thank you, Jesus.
MATTIE FAE: Tell us something, how old is he, what does he
    do?—
IVY: I'm not telling you anything, either of you, so you might
    as well—
MATTIE FAE: You have to tell us *something!*
IVY: No, I really don't.
VIOLET: Are you in love, Ivy?
IVY *(Stunned)*: I . . . I don't . . . I'm . . .

> *(She bursts into awkward laughter and exits down the second-floor hallway. Violet and Mattie Fae squeal and follow Ivy off.*
>   *Lights crossfade to the front porch as Jean zips inside. She races to the TV, turns it on, finds a channel, and sits improbably close. Bill and Steve Heidebrecht follow, dressed in dark suits and laden with paper grocery bags.)*

STEVE: No, we maintain the accounts offshore, just until we get
    approvals.
BILL: To get around approvals?

STEVE: To get around approvals until we *get* approvals. There's a lot of red tape, a lot of bureaucracy. I don't know how much you know about Florida, Florida politics—

BILL: Only what I read and that's—

STEVE: Right, right, and this kind of business in particular—

BILL: I'm sorry, what is the business again? I don't—

STEVE: You know, it's essentially security work. The situation in the Middle East is *perpetually* dangerous, so there's a tremendous amount of money involved—

BILL: Security work. You mean . . . mercenary?

(Barbara enters from the kitchen.)

BARBARA: Give. Me. The wine.

(She pulls a bottle of wine from Bill's grocery bag.)

STEVE: I think of it more like "missionary" than "mercenary."

BARBARA *(To Jean, regarding the TV)*: Is that what you were in such a hurry to get home for?

JEAN: Yeah.

BARBARA: What the hell is on TV that's so important you can't—?

JEAN: *Phantom of the Opera*, 1925. Lon Chaney.

BILL: Cool.

BARBARA: For God's sake, Jean, you can get it at any video store.

JEAN: No, but they're showing it with the scene in color restored.

BILL: Oh, no kidding, from the . . . what's that scene called again, sweetie? "The Masked Ball"?

JEAN: Yeah.

BARBARA: Let me make sure I've got this: when you threw a fit about going to the store with your father—hey. Look at me.

(She does.)

And you were so very distraught over the start time of your grandpa's funeral. Was this your concern? Getting back here in time to watch the *Phantom of the Fucking Opera?*

JEAN: I guess.

(Barbara gives Jean a withering look, exits.)

BILL *(To Steve)*: I'll take these into the kitchen.

STEVE: No, I can.

BILL: I've got it.

(Bill takes Steve's grocery bag and follows Barbara into the kitchen.)

STEVE: Movie buff?

JEAN: Yeah.

STEVE: Right, right, me too. You ever seen this?

JEAN: Huh-uh.

STEVE: It's a great one. You know Chaney designed his own makeup.

JEAN: I know.

STEVE: Apparently very painful. He ran these fishing lines from under his nostrils and pulled them up under his—

JEAN: Yeah, I know.

STEVE: You see any of the remakes? They're pretty bad.

JEAN: I've seen the one with Claude Rains.

STEVE: Right, right, pretty bad, right? Phantom's queer. That's a problem.

JEAN: I don't remember it so hot, I was just a kid.

STEVE: Yeah . . .

(Steve sits on the couch behind her. They watch the movie for a moment.)

You're not a kid anymore, I guess.

JEAN: What?

STEVE: I say you're not a kid anymore.

JEAN: No. I mean, *yeah.*

STEVE: How old are you, about, seventeen?

JEAN: Fifteen.

STEVE: Right, right. Fifteen. That's no kid.

(They watch TV.)

You're no kid. *(Beat)* You know what I was doing when I was fifteen?

JEAN: What?

STEVE: Cattle processing. You know what that is?

JEAN: It doesn't sound good.

STEVE: Slaughterhouse. Sanitation. Slaughterhouse sanitation.

JEAN: That's disgusting.

STEVE: I don't recommend it. But hey. Put food on the table. Get it?

(He sniffs the air.)

Whoa, whoa. Wait now. What's that smell?

JEAN: Food, from the kitchen.

STEVE: Nah, that's not what I'm smelling.

(He continues to sniff the air, follows his nose, until he is on the floor, above her. He smells her.)

JEAN: What are you doing?

STEVE: Do I smell what I think I smell?

JEAN: What do you smell?

STEVE: What do you think I smell?

JEAN: I think you smell food from the kitchen.

STEVE: Guess again.

(He whiffs, hard, breathing her in.)

JEAN: What are you—?
STEVE: Is that—is that pot?
JEAN: Oh. I don't know.

(She smells her sleeve.)

STEVE: You smoking pot?
JEAN: No.
STEVE: You can tell me.
JEAN: No.
STEVE: Is it just me, or is it getting hot in here?
JEAN: It's hot.
STEVE: You're hot?
JEAN: Yeah . . .
STEVE: How hot are you?
JEAN: Really hot.
STEVE: Really hot.
JEAN: Yeah.
STEVE: Yeah . . . you a little dope smoker?

(No response.)

Well then you are in luck. Because I just happen to have some really tasty shit. Because I just happen to have some really good connects. And I am going to hook you up.
JEAN: That would be great 'cause I just smoked my last bowl, and I really need to get fucked up.
STEVE: You what?
JEAN: I really need to get fucked up—
STEVE: You need to get what?
JEAN: Fucked up—
STEVE: What? You need to get fucked what?

71

(She snort-laughs, pushes him away.)

JEAN: You're bad.

STEVE: I'm just goofin' with you.

(Karen enters from the kitchen, finds Steve on the floor, looming over Jean.)

Hi, sweetheart.

KAREN: What are you doing?

STEVE: Goofin' with your niece.

KAREN: I think we're getting ready to eat.

STEVE: Right, right, I'm starving.

KAREN: Did you remember to get cigarettes?

STEVE: Damn it. *(To Jean)* Didn't I ask you what I was forgetting? I knew I was forgetting something—

KAREN: I'll have to borrow from Momma.

JEAN: I've got cigarettes.

KAREN: *You've* got cigarettes.

JEAN: Camel Lights?

STEVE: She's got our brand.

KAREN: Jean, honey, you're too young to smoke.

STEVE *(Faux stern)*: Yeah.

KAREN *(Whacks him playfully)*: Stop it now, don't encourage her—

STEVE: Hey, she's no kid—

KAREN: Can we borrow a couple of cigarettes?

JEAN: Yep-per.

(Jean gets cigarettes from her purse.)

STEVE: Now let's not encourage her—

KAREN: Oh, hush. *(Takes cigarettes)* Thanks, doll. Now stop smoking.

(Jean watches TV. Karen snuggles with Steve, speaks in a baby voice.)

Hi, doodle.
STEVE: Hey, baby.
KAREN *(In a super baby voice)*: Hi, doodle!

(Steve embraces her. They kiss. His hands wander, squeeze her ass. She giggles, then breaks it.)

Come into the backyard, I want to show you our old fort. Man, the air in here just doesn't move . . .

(She goes ahead of him. He follows, but stops . . .)

STEVE *(Privately, to Jean)*: Hook you up, later.

(. . . rubs his hand over the entirety of Jean's face. He exits.
Lights crossfade to the front porch as Charlie and Little Charles arrive.)

LITTLE CHARLES: I'm sorry, Dad.
CHARLIE: Stop apologizing to me. Hold on a second, comb your hair.

(Charlie gives Little Charles a comb.)

LITTLE CHARLES: I know Mom's mad at me.
CHARLIE: Don't worry about her.
LITTLE CHARLES: What did she say?
CHARLIE: You know your mother, she says what she says.
LITTLE CHARLES: I set the alarm. I did.
CHARLIE: I know you did.
LITTLE CHARLES: I wanted to be there.
CHARLIE: You're here now.

LITTLE CHARLES: I loved Uncle Bev, you know that—

CHARLIE: Stop apologizing.

LITTLE CHARLES: The power must've gone out. I woke up and the clock was blinking noon. That means the power went out, right?

CHARLIE: It's okay.

LITTLE CHARLES: I missed his funeral!

CHARLIE: It's a ceremony. It's ceremonial. It doesn't mean anything compared to what you have in your heart.

LITTLE CHARLES: Uncle Bev must be disappointed in me.

CHARLIE: Your Uncle Bev has got bigger and better things ahead of him. He doesn't have time for spite. He wasn't that kind of man anyway—

(Little Charles weeps.)

Hey. Little Charles. Hey. It's okay. It's okay, now . . .

LITTLE CHARLES: Just . . . it's just . . . you know, I know how things are. I know how they feel about me, and when, something like this . . . you want to be there for people, and—

CHARLIE: —shhhh—

LITTLE CHARLES: —I missed Uncle Bev's funeral, and I know how they feel about me—

CHARLIE: Who, how who feels about you? Feels what about you?

LITTLE CHARLES: All of them. I know what they say.

CHARLIE: They don't say things about you—

LITTLE CHARLES: I see how they are. I don't blame them. I'm sorry I let you down, Dad.

CHARLIE: You haven't let me down. You never let me down. Now listen here . . . you're wrong about these people, they love you. Some of them haven't gotten a chance to see what I see: a fine man, very loving, with a lot to offer. Now take this . . . *(Gives Little Charles a handkerchief)* Give me my

74

comb. Stand up straight. Look folks in the eye. And stop being so hard on yourself.

LITTLE CHARLES: I love you, Dad.

CHARLIE: Love you too, son.

(Charlie claps Little Charles on the back as they enter the living room.

Lights crossfade to the dining room as Barbara and Bill enter from the kitchen. Johnna occasionally interrupts as she moves between the kitchen and the dining room, setting the table with food.)

BILL: Jean doesn't understand all this. You think she has any concept—?

BARBARA: *Phantom of the Opera*—

BILL: Do you remember what it was like to be fourteen?

BARBARA: She's old enough to exhibit a little character. But then I guess that's something you normally learn from your parents.

BILL: That's a shot across my bow, right? I missed something.

BARBARA: Really? Instilling character: our burden, as parents.

BILL: I got that part.

BARBARA: And you really haven't been much of a parent lately, so it's tough to expect—

BILL: Just because you and I are struggling with this Gordian knot doesn't make me any less of a—

BARBARA: Nice, "Gordian knot," but her little fourteen-year-old self might view it differently, might consider it "abandonment"—

BILL: Oh, come on—

BARBARA: Maybe she views her father as "absent," or maybe "not present," or perhaps even "a son-of-a-bitch."

BILL: Jean's a little more sophisticated than that, don't you think?

BARBARA: Pretty fucking sophisticated, the restored whatever from *Phantom of the Opera*, I know that makes your dick hard—

BILL: Barbara—
BARBARA: Precocious little shit—
BILL: I'm not defending her.

BARBARA *(Voice rising)*: I'm not blaming her, because I don't expect her to act any differently when her father is a selfish son-of-a-bitch!

BILL *(Voice rising)*: I'm on your side. How can we fight when I'm on your side? Barbara . . . Barbara, settle down!

BARBARA: Be a father! Help me!
BILL: I am her father, goddamn it!—
BARBARA: Her father *in absentia,* her father in name only!—
BILL: I have not forsook my responsibilities!—
BARBARA: It's "forsaken," big shot!
BILL: Actually, "forsook" is *also* an acceptable usage!—
BARBARA: Oh, *"forsook"* you and the horse you rode in on!
BILL: So we need to fight on your terms then: on topic one moment, and whimsical insults the next, all of it when it suits you—
BARBARA: We covered this around Year Three, Bill: that you're the Master of Space and Time and I'm a spastic Pomeranian.
BILL: That's not fair.
BARBARA: I'm sick of being fair! I've seen where being fair gets me! I'm sick of the whole notion of the enduring female. GROW UP! 'Cause while you're going through your fifth puberty, the world is falling apart and I can't handle it! More importantly, your kid can't handle it!
BILL: Our kid is just trying to deal with this goddamn madhouse you've dragged her into.
BARBARA: This madhouse is my home.
BILL: Think about that statement for a second, why don't you?
BARBARA: Jean is here with me because this is a family event.
BILL: Jean's here with you because she's a buffer between you and the shrill insanity of your mother.

BARBARA: Y'know, you'd have a lot more credibility if you had any credibility.

BILL: You can't resist, can you?

BARBARA: You're a pretty easy mark.

BILL: You're so goddamn self-righteous, you know? You're so—

BARBARA: Surely you must've known when you started porking Pippi Longstocking you were due for a little self-righteousness, just a smidgen of indignation on my part—

BILL: Maybe I split because of it.

BARBARA: Is this your confession, then, when you finally unload all—?

BILL: You're thoughtful, Barbara, but you're not open. You're passionate, but you're hard. You're a good, decent, funny, wonderful woman, and I love you, but you're a pain in the ass.

(Lights up on the entire house:
Bill exits to the porch, gathers himself.
Karen and Steve reenter, run into Barbara in the sitting room.
Mattie Fae descends the stairs to the living room where Jean, Charlie and Little Charles watch TV.
Violet and Ivy reenter the second-floor landing.)

JOHNNA: Dinner's ready.

STEVE: I told you, smoke a cigarette and the food comes—

KAREN *(To Barbara)*: When's the last time someone mowed the yard around here?

MATTIE FAE: Well, look who decided to show up. I'm sorry we woke you, sweetheart.

LITTLE CHARLES: Mom, I'm so sorry—

IVY: I'm serious, if you say anything—

VIOLET: You didn't say I couldn't tell people—

IVY: I'm telling you now.

77

BARBARA: Hm?

KAREN: I just showed Steve our old fort, have you been out there?

BARBARA: No, I haven't—

STEVE: Barb, would you consider me uncouth if I removed my suit jacket?

KAREN: Are you okay?

BARBARA: Yeah, I'm fine.

STEVE: Barbara, can I . . . ?

BARBARA: Yeah, sure.

KAREN: Poor thing, you've had a long few days, haven't you?

STEVE: Sure she has.

KAREN: I know how I get during these times, I think, "I couldn't eat a bite," but then you put a plate of hot food in front of me and suddenly I'm starving.

MATTIE FAE: I'm sure you are—

CHARLIE: He's here now and that's all that matters.

MATTIE FAE: It's really not all that matters—

LITTLE CHARLES: The electricity must have gone out, I woke up and the clock—

MATTIE FAE: Don't go through it all, Little Charles. There's no need to go through all—

CHARLIE: Honey, the boy's trying to tell you he's sorry—

MATTIE FAE: Stop making excuses for him, he's thirty-seven years old—

CHARLIE: Please let's not have this argument now.

MATTIE FAE: I'm not arguing.

LITTLE CHARLES: I know I let you down, Mom—

VIOLET: Why are you so worked up? You're seeing someone, I think that's great—

IVY: Don't you dare—

VIOLET: You'd think you might be happy to tell your family some good news, on a day like today?—

IVY: It's nobody's business.

VIOLET: Folks only want what's best for you.

IVY: It's nobody's business!

VIOLET: Why should I do you any favors?

IVY: Why not? Why *wouldn't* you?

VIOLET: You wouldn't even try on my dress—

IVY: I'm not bargaining with you!

VIOLET: You're so melodramatic—

(A pause, as Barbara seems to take them in for the first time.)

BARBARA: You're right. Let's eat.

STEVE: Let's eat!

(They cross from the kitchen into the dining room.)

MATTIE FAE: What else is new?

CHARLIE: You behave yourself, there's more important things—

MATTIE FAE: I'm not talking about this anymore, I'm ready to eat. Did you bring my casserole in from—?

CHARLIE: No, I'll get it now.

MATTIE FAE: You let my casserole sit for an hour inside a hot car?—

CHARLIE: I'll get it, I'll get it—

LITTLE CHARLES: *I'll* get it.

(Little Charles exits the house.)

IVY: I'm going downstairs to eat now because you are impossible.

VIOLET *(Sarcastic)*: I'm sorry to be so impossible, it's been kind of a tough day—

IVY: Tough on everybody, Mom.

(Ivy heads downstairs, enters the living room as Mattie Fae and Charlie join Barbara, Karen, Steve and Johnna in the dining room. They gradually take their seats. Bill reenters from the porch, crosses into the living room.)

79

KAREN: This just looks lovely. *(To Johnna)* Did you do all this?

MATTIE FAE: What a pretty table!

JOHNNA: Mm-hm.

BARBARA: She does it all, this one.

STEVE: The chicken looks tasty, doesn't it?—

MATTIE FAE: Do we have enough seats?

BARBARA: I think so . . .

CHARLIE: Where do you want to sit?

MATTIE FAE: This'll be fine, right here—

KAREN: Sit by me, honey.

STEVE: Okie-doke.

BARBARA: Who gets stuck with Jean at the kid's table?

MATTIE FAE: We'll put Mr. Little Charles there.

CHARLIE: Are you serious?

KAREN: Nooo, now—

BILL: Jean. Time to eat.

JEAN: I don't suppose it would be okay if I ate out here.

BILL: You suppose right.

IVY: Did I hear Little Charles?

BILL: Yeah, I think so—

JEAN: You're just gonna stick me at the kid's table anyway.

BILL: I'm not in the mood for this right now, okay?

IVY: Is he—do you know where he is?

BILL: I think he went outside for something—

(Ivy exits to the front porch. Jean stomps toward the dining room. Bill stops her.)

Why are you giving me all this attitude?

JEAN: I'm not.

BILL: You do realize your mother needs you at your best right now.

JEAN: Mom's not the one crawling up my ass.

BILL: Never mind. Wash up for dinner.

JEAN: "Wash up"? I'm not performing surgery.

MATTIE FAE: Who else is going to sit there? Do *you* want to sit there?

CHARLIE: He's going to know you're trying to punish him—

JOHNNA: I can sit there, it's okay.

MATTIE FAE: After you went to all the trouble of cooking this fabulous meal—?

JOHNNA: I don't mind.

(Jean and Bill enter the dining room.)

(As the family continues to settle in for the meal, lights shift again: up on the front porch. Ivy greets Little Charles as he returns with Mattie Fae's casserole.)

IVY: Hey.

LITTLE CHARLES: Hi.

IVY: Are you okay?

LITTLE CHARLES: Not really.

IVY: They said you overslept.

LITTLE CHARLES: I don't know, maybe I purposely accidentally overslept. I don't know. I'm so sorry—

IVY: Please.

LITTLE CHARLES: I know you've had one of the worst days of your life and I'm just sorry if I made it any—

IVY: Stop. We don't have to do that with each other.

(She embraces him, kisses him . . .)

LITTLE CHARLES: You're breaking our rule.

IVY: They're on to me.

LITTLE CHARLES: What?

IVY: Not us, just me. I told them I was seeing someone. I didn't tell them who. I just wanted you to know, in case there were questions . . .

LITTLE CHARLES: All right . . . I mentioned New York to Mom. Only, you know, that I was considering a move.

IVY: She told me.

LITTLE CHARLES: She was typically approving, I bet . . .

IVY: But you know what? I think it helps, just letting them know, piece by piece.

(He stares at her.)

What?

(He stares, smiles.)

Charles . . .

LITTLE CHARLES: I adore you.

(Lights crossfade to the dining room. Seated around the table: Barbara, Bill, Mattie Fae, Charlie, Karen and Steve. Jean and Johnna sit at the kid's table. The men have all removed their suit coats.)

MATTIE FAE: This food's going to get cold.

BARBARA *(Calling out)*: Mom?! Let's eat.

CHARLIE: Will you pass the casserole, please?

MATTIE FAE: *My* casserole's coming.

CHARLIE: I'll eat some of yours, too—

BILL: Can I pour anyone some wine?

KAREN: Yes, please.   STEVE: Sure, I'll have some—

(Little Charles enters with Mattie Fae's casserole.)

MATTIE FAE: There he is. I wanted to put you at the kid's table, but they wouldn't let me.

LITTLE CHARLES: That would've been okay. Where do you want this?

MATTIE FAE: Anywhere's fine.

(Ad-lib greetings, hugs, handshakes, Karen's introduction of Steve, etc. Ivy slips in and takes her seat.
Little Charles drops Mattie Fae's casserole. It lands with a sickening "splat" on the dining room floor.)

LITTLE CHARLES: Oh Jesus!—	BILL: Whoops.
MATTIE FAE: Goddamn it!—	BARBARA: That's too bad—
LITTLE CHARLES: Oh Jesus	
no!—	STEVE: O-pah!
MATTIE FAE: You *goofball!*	KAREN: Can it be saved?

(Johnna goes to the kitchen for paper towels, a wet rag, etc.)

MATTIE FAE: You goddamn clumsy *goofball!*

LITTLE CHARLES: Mom, I'm	CHARLIE: All right, all right,
so sorry—	nobody's hurt.

(Little Charles helps Johnna clean up the mess.)

MATTIE FAE: What about me? *I'm* hurt.
CHARLIE: You're not hurt.
LITTLE CHARLES: Mom, Jesus, I'm sorry—
IVY: It's just an accident.
MATTIE FAE: That's *my* casserole!
CHARLIE: Let it go, Mattie Fae.
STEVE: It's not a party until someone spills something.
CHARLIE: Jean, you didn't get any chicken.

BARBARA: No, she won't—	JEAN: I don't eat meat.

CHARLIE: You don't eat meat.
STEVE: Good for you.

CHARLIE: "Don't eat meat." Okay. Who wants chicken? Here, Little Charles, get some chicken.

MATTIE FAE: Just put it on his plate for him or he's liable to burn the house down.

CHARLIE: All right, Mattie Fae.

(Violet enters with the framed photograph of her and Beverly.)

VIOLET: Barb . . . will you put this—?

BARBARA: Yeah, sure . . .

(Barbara takes the photograph, places it on the sideboard.)

MATTIE FAE: That's nice.

KAREN: That's sweet.

STEVE: Very nice, yes.

IVY: The table's lovely.

BARBARA: Johnna did it all.

JEAN: Yayyy, Johnna—

VIOLET: I see you gentlemen have all stripped down to your shirt fronts. I thought we were having a funeral dinner, not a cockfight.

(An awkward moment. The men glumly put their suit coats back on.)

(Taking her seat) Someone should probably say grace.

(All look to one another.)

Barbara? Will you . . . ?

BARBARA: No, I don't think so.

VIOLET: Oh now, it's no big—

BARBARA: Uncle Charlie should say grace. He's the patriarch around here now.

CHARLIE: I am? Oh, I guess I am.

VIOLET: By default.
CHARLIE: Okay. *(Clears his throat)* Dear Lord . . .

(All bow their heads, clasp hands.)

We ask that you watch over this family in this sad time, O Lord . . . that you bless this good woman and keep her in your, in your . . . grace.

(A cell phone rings, playing the theme from Sanford and Son. *Steve quickly digs through his pockets, finds the phone, checks the caller ID.)*

STEVE: I'm sorry, I have to take this.

(Steve hustles out to talk on the phone.)

CHARLIE: We ask that you watch over Beverly, too, as he, as he . . . as he, as he, as he makes his journey.

We thank thee, O Lord, that we are able to join together to pay tribute to this fine man, in his house, with his beautiful family, his three beautiful daughters. We are truly blessed in our, our fellowship, our togetherness, our . . . our fellowship.

Thank thee for the food, O Lord, that we can share this food and replenish our bodies with . . . with nourishment. We ask that you help us . . . get better. Be better. Be better people.

(Steve reenters, snapping his phone shut.)

We recognize, now more than ever, the power, the, the . . . joy of family. And we ask that you bless and watch over this family. Amen.
MATTIE FAE: Amen.
STEVE: Amen. Sorry, folks.

BILL: Let's eat.

(They begin to eat.)

VIOLET: Barbara, you have any use for that sideboard.
BARBARA: Hm?
VIOLET: That sideboard there, you have any interest in that?
BARBARA: This? Well . . . no. I mean, why?
VIOLET: I'm getting rid of a lot of this stuff and I thought you
 might want that sideboard.

BARBARA: No, Mom, I . . . I wouldn't have any way to get that to Boulder.	KAREN: Really pretty.

VIOLET: Mm. Maybe Ivy'll take it.
IVY: No, I have something like that, remember, from the—
BARBARA: What are you getting rid of?
VIOLET: All of it, I'm clearing all this stuff out of here. I want
 to have a brand-new everything.
BARBARA: I. I guess I'm just sort of . . . not prepared to talk
 about your stuff.
VIOLET: Suit yourself.
STEVE: This food is just spectacular.

KAREN: It's so good—	LITTLE CHARLES: Yes, it is—

IVY: You like your food, Mom?
VIOLET: I haven't tried much of it, yet—
BARBARA: Johnna cooked this whole meal by herself.
VIOLET: Hm? What?
BARBARA: I say Johnna cooked this whole meal by—
VIOLET: 'Swhat she's paid for.

(A silent moment.)

You all did know she's getting paid, right?

CHARLIE: Jean, so I'm curious, when you say you don't eat meat . . .

JEAN: Yeah?

CHARLIE: You mean you don't eat meat of any kind?

JEAN: Right.   BARBARA: No, she, hm-mm . . .

CHARLIE: And is that for health reasons, or . . . ?

JEAN: When you eat meat, you ingest an animal's fear.

VIOLET: Ingest what? Its fur?

JEAN: Fear.

VIOLET *(Snickers)*: I thought she said—

CHARLIE: Its fear. How do you do that? You can't eat fear.

JEAN: Sure you can. I mean even if you don't sort of think of it spiritually, what happens to *you*, when you feel afraid? Doesn't your body produce all sorts of chemical reactions?

CHARLIE: Does it?

LITTLE CHARLES: It does.

IVY: Yes.

LITTLE CHARLES: Adrenaline, and, and—

JEAN: Your body goes through this whole chemical process when it experiences fear—

LITTLE CHARLES: —yep, and cortisol—

JEAN: —particularly like strong mortal fear, you know when you sweat and your heart races—

LITTLE CHARLES: —*oh* yeah—

CHARLIE: Okay, sure.

JEAN: Do you think an animal experiences fear?

STEVE: You bet it does.

JEAN: So when you eat an animal, you're eating all that fear it felt when it was slaughtered to make food.

CHARLIE: Wow.

STEVE: Right, right, I used to work in a processing factory and there's a lot of fear flying around that place—

CHARLIE: God, you mean I've been eating fear, what, three times a day for sixty years?

MATTIE FAE: This one won't have a meal unless there's meat in it.

CHARLIE: I guess it was the way I was raised, but it just doesn't seem like a legitimate meal unless it has some meat somewhere—

MATTIE FAE: If I make a pasta dish of some kind, he'll just be like, "Okay, that was good for an appetizer, now where's the meat?"

VIOLET: "Where's the meat?" Isn't that some TV commercial, the old lady say, "Where's the meat?"

KAREN: "Beef." "Where's the beef?"

VIOLET *(Screeching)*: *"Where's the meat?!" "Where's the meat?!" "Where's the meat?!"*

(Everyone freezes, a little stunned.)

CHARLIE: I sure thought the services were lovely.

KAREN: Yes, weren't they?—

STEVE: Preacher did a fine job.

VIOLET *(Sticking her hand out, flat, waggling it back and forth)*: Ehhhhh! I give it a . . . *(Repeats gesture)* Ehhhhh!

KAREN: Really? I thought it was—

BARBARA: Great, now we get some dramatic criticism—

VIOLET: I would've preferred an open casket.

BARBARA: That just wasn't possible, Mom.

VIOLET: That today's the send-off Bev should've got if he died around 1974. Lots of talk about poetry, teaching. Well, he hadn't written any poetry to speak of since '65 and he never liked teaching worth a damn. Nobody talked about the good stuff. Man was a world-class alcoholic, more'n fifty years. Nobody told the story about that night he got wrangled into giving a talk at a TU alumni dinner . . . *(Laughs)* Drank a whole bottle of rum, Ron Bocoy White Rum—I don't know why I remember that—and got up to give this talk . . . and he fouled himself! Comes back to our table with this huge—

BARBARA: Yeah, I can't imagine why no one told *that* story.

VIOLET: He didn't get invited back to any more alumni dinners, I'll tell you that!

(She cracks up.)

STEVE: You know, I don't know much about poetry, but I thought his poems were extraordinary. *(To Bill)* And your reading was very fine.

BILL: Thank you.

VIOLET *(To Steve)*: Who *are* you?

KAREN: Mom, this is my fiancé, Steve, I introduced you at the church.

STEVE: Steve Heidebrecht.

VIOLET: Hide-the-what?

STEVE: Heidebrecht.

VIOLET: Hide-a-burrr . . . German, you're a German.

STEVE: Well, German-Irish, really, I—

VIOLET: That's peculiar, Karen, to bring a date to your father's funeral. I know the poetry was good, but I wouldn't have really considered it date material—

BARBARA: Jesus.

KAREN: He's not a date, he's my fiancé. We're getting married on New Year's.

CHARLIE: Man, these potatoes are—

KAREN: In Miami, I hope you can make it.

VIOLET: I don't really see that happening, do you?

KAREN: I—

VIOLET: Steve. That right? *Steve?*

STEVE: Yes, ma'am.

VIOLET: You ever been married before?

KAREN: That's personal.

STEVE: I don't mind. Yes, ma'am, I have.

VIOLET: More'n once?

STEVE: Three times, actually, three times before this—

VIOLET: You should pretty much have it down by now, then.

STEVE *(Laughs)*: Right, right—

VIOLET *(To Mattie Fae)*: I had that one pegged, didn't I? I mean, look at him, you can tell he's been married—

KAREN: I took Steve out to show him the old fort and it's gone!

IVY: That's been gone for years.

KAREN: That made me so sad!

BILL: What is this now?

KAREN: Our old fort, where we used to play Cowboys and Indians.

IVY: Daddy said rats were getting in there—

VIOLET: Karen! Shame on you!

KAREN: Hm?

VIOLET: Don't you know not to say "Cowboys and Indians"? You played Cowboys and Native Americans. Right, Barb?

BARBARA: What'd you take?

VIOLET: Hm?

BARBARA: What did you take? What pills did you take?

VIOLET: Lemme alone—

(Charlie drops his head, appears distressed.)

CHARLIE: Uh-oh . . .

MATTIE FAE: What is it?

CHARLIE: UH-OH!

MATTIE FAE: What's the matter?

(Rising panic . . .)

LITTLE CHARLES: Dad—?   IVY: You okay, Uncle—?

CHARLIE: I just got a big bite of fear!

(Everyone laughs.)

I'm shakin' in my boots!

(Laughter, ad-libs, etc. Charlie digs into his plate ravenously.)

Fear never tasted so good.

(He winks at Jean.)

STEVE *(Laughing)*: Right, right, it's pretty good once you get used to the taste.

BARBARA *(Teasing)*: I catch her eating a cheeseburger every now and again.

JEAN: I do not!

BARBARA: Double cheeseburger with bacon, extra fear.

JEAN: Mom, you are such a liar!

(More laughter.)

VIOLET *(Staring intensely at Jean)*: Y'know . . . if I ever called my mom a liar? She would've knocked my goddamn head off my shoulders.

(Silence.)

Bill, I see you've gone through much of Beverly's office.

BILL: Not all of it, but—

VIOLET: Find any hidden treasure?

BILL: Not exactly, but it appears he was working on some new poetry.

KAREN: Really?

BILL: I found a couple of notebooks that had—

VIOLET: You girls know there's a will.

BARBARA: Mom . . .

VIOLET: We took care of that some time back, but—

BARBARA: Mom, really, we don't want to talk about this now—

VIOLET: I want to talk about it. What about what I want to talk about, that count for anything?

BARBARA: It's just—

VIOLET: Bev made some good investments if you can believe it, and we had things covered for you girls, but he and I talked it over after some years passed and decided to change things, leave everything to me. We never got around to taking care of it legally, but you should know he meant to leave everything to me. Leave the money to me.

BARBARA: Okay.

VIOLET: Okay? *(Checks in with Ivy, Karen)* Okay?

IVY: Okay.

VIOLET: Karen? Okay?

(Uncertain, Karen looks to Steve, then Barbara.)

BARBARA: Okay.

KAREN: Okay.

VIOLET: Okay. But now some of this furniture, some of this old shit you can just have. I don't want it, got no use for it. Maybe I should have an auction.

MATTIE FAE: Sure, an auction's a fine idea—

VIOLET: Some things, though, like the silver, that's worth a pretty penny. But if you like I'll sell it to you, cheaper'n I might get in an auction.

BARBARA: Or you might never get around to the auction and then we can just have it for free after you die.

IVY: Barbara . . .

(Pause. Violet coolly studies Barbara.)

VIOLET: You might at that.

LITTLE CHARLES: Excuse me, Bill? I'm wondering, this writing you found, these poems—?

VIOLET: Where are you living now, Bill? You want this old sideboard?

BILL: I beg your pardon.

VIOLET: You and Barbara are separated, right? Or you divorced already?

(Another silence.)

BILL: We're separated.

VIOLET *(To Barbara)*: Thought you could slip that one by me, didn't you?

BARBARA: What is the matter with you?

VIOLET: Nobody slips anything by me. I know what's what. Your father thought he's slipping one by me, right? No way. I'm sorry you two're having trouble . . . maybe you can work it out. Bev'n I separated a couple of times, 'course, though we didn't call it that—

BARBARA: Please, help us to benefit from an illustration of your storybook marriage—

VIOLET: Truth is, sweetheart, you can't compete with a younger woman, there's no way to compete. One of those unfair things in life. Is there a younger woman involved?

BARBARA: You've already said enough on this subject, I think—

BILL: Yes. There's a younger woman.

VIOLET: Ah . . . y'see? Odds're against you there, babe.

IVY: Mom believes women don't grow more attractive with age.

KAREN: Oh, I disagree, I—

VIOLET: I didn't say they "don't grow more attractive," I said they get ugly. And it's not really a matter of opinion, Karen dear. You've only just started to prove it yourself.

CHARLIE: You're in rare form today, Vi.

VIOLET: The day calls for it, doesn't it? What form would you have me in?

CHARLIE: I just don't understand why you're so adversarial.

VIOLET: I'm just truth-telling. *(Cutting her eyes to Barbara)* Some people get antagonized by the truth.

CHARLIE: Everyone here loves you, dear.

VIOLET: You think you can *shame* me, Charlie? Blow it out your ass.

BARBARA: Three days ago . . . I had to identify my father's corpse. And now I sit here and listen to you viciously attack each and every member of this family—

(Violet rises, her voice booming.)

VIOLET: "Attack my family"?! You ever been attacked in your sweet spoiled life?! Tell her 'bout attacks, Mattie Fae, tell her what an attack looks like!

MATTIE FAE: Vi, please—

IVY: Settle down, Mom—

VIOLET: Stop telling me to settle down, goddamn it! I'm not a goddamn invalid! I don't need to be abided, do I?! Am I already passed over?!

MATTIE FAE: Honey—

VIOLET *(Points to Mattie Fae)*: This woman came to my rescue when one of my dear mother's many gentlemen friends was attacking me, with a claw hammer! This woman has dents in her skull from hammer blows! You think you been attacked?! What do you know about life on these Plains? What do you know about hard times?

BARBARA: I know you had a rotten childhood, Mom. Who didn't?

VIOLET: You DON'T know! You do NOT know! None of you know, 'cept this woman right here and that man we buried today! Sweet girl, sweet Barbara, my heart breaks for every time you ever felt pain. I wish I coulda shielded you from it. But if you think for a solitary second you can fathom the pain that man endured in his natural life, you got another thing coming. Do you know where your father lived from age four till about ten? Do you?

(No one responds.)

Do you?!

BARBARA: No.

IVY: No.

VIOLET: *In a Pontiac sedan.* With his mother, his father, in a fucking car! Now what else do you want to say about your rotten childhood? That's the crux of the biscuit: we lived

94

too hard, then rose too high. We sacrificed everything and we did it all for you. Your father and I were the first in our families to finish high school and he wound up an award-winning poet. You girls, given a college education, taken for granted no doubt, and where'd *you* wind up? *(Jabs a finger at Karen)* Whadda *you* do? *(Jabs a finger at Ivy)* Whadda *you* do? *(Jabs a finger at Barbara)* Who're *you*? Jesus, you worked as hard as us, you'd all be president. You never had real problems so you got to make all your problems yourselves.

BARBARA: Why are you screaming at us?

VIOLET: Just time we had some truth's told 'round here's all. Damn fine day, tell the truth.

CHARLIE: Well, the truth is . . . I'm getting full.

STEVE: Amen.

JOHNNA: There's dessert, too.

KAREN: I saw her making those pies. They looked so good.

(Little Charles suddenly stands.)

LITTLE CHARLES: I have a truth to tell.

VIOLET: It speaks.

(Little Charles looks to Ivy.)

IVY *(Softly pleading)*: Nooo, nooo—

CHARLIE: What is it, son?

LITTLE CHARLES: I have a truth.

(Silence.)

MATTIE FAE: Little Charles . . . ?

LITTLE CHARLES: I . . .

IVY *(Almost to herself)*: Charles, not like this, please . . .

LITTLE CHARLES: The truth is, I . . . I forgot to set the clock. This morning. The power didn't go out, I just . . . forgot to set the clock. Sorry, Mom. I'm sorry, everyone. Excuse me . . . I . . . I.

(He leaves the dining room, exits the house . . . pauses on the porch, exits.)

VIOLET: Scintillating.

(Charlie turns to Mattie Fae, confused.)

MATTIE FAE: I gave up a long time ago . . . Little Charles is your project.

IVY *(Near tears)*: Charles. His name is Charles.

(The family eats in silence. Violet pats Ivy's wrists.)

VIOLET: Poor Ivy. Poor thing.
IVY: Please, Mom . . .
VIOLET: Poor baby.
IVY: Please . . .
VIOLET: She's always had a feeling for the underdog.
IVY: Don't be mean to me right now, okay?
VIOLET: Everyone's got this idea I'm mean, all of a sudden.
IVY: *Please*, Momma.
VIOLET: I told you, I'm just telling the—
BARBARA: You're a drug addict.
VIOLET: That is the truth! That's what I'm getting at! I, everybody listen . . . I am a drug addict. I am addicted to drugs, pills, 'specially downers. *(Pulls a bottle of pills from her pocket, holds them up)* Y'see these little blue babies? These are my best fucking friends and they never let me down. Try to get 'em away from me and I'll eat you alive.
BARBARA: Gimme those goddamn pills—
VIOLET: I'll eat you alive, girl!

(Barbara lunges at the bottle of pills. She and Violet wrestle with it. Bill and Ivy try to restrain Barbara. Mattie Fae tries to restrain Violet. Others rise, ad-lib.)

STEVE: Holy shit—
IVY: Barbara, stop it!—
CHARLIE: Hey, now, c'mon!—
KAREN: Oh God—

(*Violet wins, wrests the pills away from Barbara. Bill pulls Barbara back into her seat. Violet shakes the pill bottle, taunting Barbara. Barbara snaps, screams, lunges again, grabs Violet by the hair, pulls her up, toppling chairs. They crash through the house, pursued by the family. Pandemonium. Screaming. Barbara strangles Violet. With great effort, Bill and Charlie pry the two women apart. Mattie Fae and Johnna rush to Violet, tend to her.*)

VIOLET (*Crying*): Goddamn you . . . goddamn you, Barb . . .
BARBARA: SHUT UP!
    (*To the others*) Okay. Pill raid. Johnna, help me in the kitchen. Bill, take Ivy and Jean upstairs. (*To Ivy*) You remember how to do this, right?
IVY: Yeah . . .
BARBARA (*To Jean*): Everything. Go through everything, every counter, every drawer, every shoe box. Nothing's too personal. Anything even looks suspicious, throw it in a box and we can sort it out later. You understand?
CHARLIE: What should we do?
BARBARA: Get Mom some black coffee and a wet towel and listen to her bullshit. Karen, call Dr. Burke.
KAREN: What do you want me to say?
BARBARA: Tell him we got a sick woman here.
VIOLET: You can't do this! This is *my* house! This is *my* house!
BARBARA: You don't get it, do you? (*With a burst of adrenaline, she strides to Violet, towers over her*) I'M RUNNING THINGS NOW!

(*Blackout.*)

ACT THREE

SCENE 1

The window shades have all been removed. Nighttime is now free to encroach.

   At rise: the three sisters in the study. They share a bottle of whiskey. An inflatable mattress, covered with a thin sheet, now lies on the study floor.

   Elsewhere in the house: a game of spades in the dining room—Charlie and Mattie Fae versus Jean and Steve. Little Charles sits by himself in the living room, watching TV. Bill sorts through paperwork on the porch. Violet, pensive, wearing a robe, her hair wrapped in a towel, sits at the window on the second-floor landing.

KAREN: The doctor really thinks she needs to go to an institution? *Does she need to go?* Did he examine her?

BARBARA: Dr. Burke says she may be brain-damaged. "Slightly brain-damaged." I told him he was "slightly incompetent" and I hoped some day soon he'd be "slightly dead." He claims not to know she was taking so much. That's why he's eager to put her away, he's afraid of a malpractice suit. I told him I was considering it. Irresponsible shithead—

KAREN: Why did he write so many prescriptions? Doesn't he know—?

BARBARA: It's not just him; she's got a doctor in every port—

IVY: Here's how she does it: she sees a doctor for back spasms and gets a prescription. Day or two later she goes back, says she lost her pills and he writes her another one. Then next week she pulls a muscle, more pills, then the dosage is wrong, more pills, over and over, until she makes one too many trips and he says I'm not prescribing anymore. And she pulls a sheaf of prescription receipts out of her purse and says, "I'll go to the AMA and have your ass in court for over-prescribing me." She genuinely threatens these men and they give in to her.

BARBARA *(To Ivy)*: You knew this was going on again?

(Ivy shrugs.)

Different tactic today, just at her wounded best, this wilting hothouse flower. Which made me look like Bette Davis. I tried to goad her into it, you know, "C'mon, Mom, give him your speech about the Greatest Generation. Tell him about the claw hammer." I was like that guy in the cartoon with the frog that only sings for him.

IVY: It wouldn't have done any good, Dr. Burke's part of the same generation.

BARBARA: "Greatest Generation," my ass. Are they really considering *all* the generations? Maybe there are some generations from the *Iron Age* that could compete. And what makes them so great anyway? Because they were poor and hated Nazis? Who doesn't fucking hate Nazis?! You remember when we checked her in the psych ward, that stunt she pulled?

IVY: Which time?

KAREN: I wasn't there.

BARBARA: Big speech, she's getting clean, this sacrifice she's making for her family, and—

IVY: Right, she's let her *family* down but now she wants to prove she's a good family member—

BARBARA: She smuggled Darvocet into the psych ward . . . *in her vagina*. There's your Greatest Generation for you. She made this speech to us while she was clenching a bottle of pills in her cooch, for God's sake.

KAREN: God, I've never heard that story.

IVY: Did you just say "cooch"?

BARBARA: The phrase "Mom's pussy" seems a bit gauche.

IVY: You're a little more comfortable with "cooch," are you?

BARBARA: What word should I use to describe our mother's vagina?

IVY: I don't know, but—

BARBARA: "Mom's beaver"? "Mother's box"?

IVY: Oh God—

KAREN: Barbara!

(Laughter, finally dying out.)

I'm sorry about you and Bill.

IVY: Me, too, Barb.

BARBARA: If I had my way, you never would've known.

KAREN: Do you think it's a temporary thing, or . . . ?

BARBARA: Who knows? We've been married a long time.

KAREN: That's one thing about Mom and Dad. You have to tip your cap to anyone who can stay married that long.

IVY: Karen. He killed himself.

KAREN: Yeah, but still.

BARBARA: Is there something going on between you and Little Charles?

IVY: I don't know that I'm comfortable talking about that.

BARBARA: Because you know he is our first cousin.

IVY: Give me a break.

KAREN: You know you shouldn't consider children.

IVY: I'm almost forty-five, Karen, I put those thoughts behind me a long time ago. Anyway, I had a hysterectomy year before last.

KAREN: Why?

IVY: Cervical cancer.

KAREN: I didn't know that.

BARBARA: Neither did I.

IVY: I didn't tell anyone except Charles. That's where it started between him and me.

BARBARA: Why not? Why wouldn't you tell anyone?

IVY: And hear those comments from Mom for the rest of my life? She doesn't need any more excuses to treat me like some damaged thing.

BARBARA: You might have told us.

IVY: You weren't going to tell us about you and Bill.

BARBARA: That's different.

IVY: Why? Because it's you, and not me?

BARBARA: No, because divorce is an embarrassing public admission of defeat. Cancer's fucking cancer, you can't help that. We're your sisters. We might've given you some comfort.

IVY: I just don't feel that connection very keenly.

KAREN: I feel very connected, to both of you.

IVY (Amused): We never see you, you're never around, you haven't been around for—

KAREN: But I still feel that connection!

IVY: You think if you tether yourself to this place in mind only, you don't need to actually appear.

KAREN: You know me that well.

IVY: No, and that's my point. I can't perpetuate these myths of family or sisterhood anymore. We're all just people, some of us accidentally connected by genetics, a random selection of cells. Nothing more.

BARBARA: When did you get so cynical?

IVY: That's funny coming from you.

BARBARA: Bitter, sure, but "random selection of cells"?

IVY: Maybe my cynicism flowered with the realization that the obligation of caring for our parents was mine alone.

BARBARA: Don't give me that. I participated in every god-damn—

IVY: Until you had enough and got out, you and Karen.

BARBARA: I had my own family to think about.

IVY: That's a cheap excuse. As if by having a child you were alleviated of all responsibility.

BARBARA: So now I'm being criticized for procreating.

IVY: I'm not criticizing. Do what you want. You did, Karen did.

BARBARA: And if you didn't, that's not my fault.

IVY: That's right, so don't lay this sister thing on me now, all right? I don't buy it. I haven't bought it for a long time. When I leave here and leave for good I won't feel any more guilty than you two did.

KAREN: Who says we don't?

BARBARA: Are you leaving here?

IVY: Charles and I are going to New York.

(Barbara bursts out laughing.)

BARBARA: What the hell are you going to do in New York?

IVY: We have plans.

BARBARA: Like what?

IVY: None of your business.

BARBARA: You can't just go to New York.

IVY: This isn't whimsy. This isn't fleeting. This is unlike anything I've ever felt, for anybody. Charles and I have something rare, and extraordinary, something very few people ever have.

KAREN: Which is what?

IVY: Understanding.

BARBARA: What about Mom?

IVY: What about her?

BARBARA: You feel comfortable leaving Mom here?

IVY: Do you?

(No response.)

You think she was difficult while Dad was alive? Think about what it's going to be like now. You can't imagine the cumulative effect, after a month, after a year, after many years. You can't imagine. And even if you could, you can only imagine for yourself, for yourself, the favorite.

BARBARA: Christ, Mom pulled that on me the other day about Dad, that I was his favorite.

IVY: Well . . . that's not true. You weren't his favorite. I was. You're Mom's favorite.

BARBARA: *What?*

KAREN: Thanks, Ivy.

IVY: You don't think so? Good God, Barb, I've lived my life by that standard.

BARBARA: She said Dad was heartbroken when we moved to Boulder—

IVY: Mom was heartbroken, not Dad. She was convinced you left to get away from her.

KAREN: If you were Daddy's favorite, you must take his suicide kind of personally.

IVY: Daddy killed himself for his own reasons.

BARBARA: And what were those reasons?

IVY: I won't presume.

BARBARA: Aren't you angry with him?

IVY: No. He's accountable to no one but himself. If he's better off now, and I don't doubt he is, who are we to begrudge him that?

BARBARA: *His daughters.*

KAREN: *Yeah*—

BARBARA: And I'm fucking furious. The selfish son-of-a-bitch, his silence, his melancholy . . . he could have, for me, for us, for all of us, he could have helped us, included us, talked to us.

IVY: You might not have liked what you heard. What if the truth of the matter is that Beverly Weston never liked you? That he never liked any of us, never had any special feeling of any kind for his children?

BARBARA: You know that's not true.

IVY: Do I? How? Do *you*?

KAREN: You said you were his favorite.

IVY: Only because he recognized a kindred spirit.

BARBARA: Mm, sorry, but your little theory, your "accidental genetics," that doesn't fly, not with me. I believe he had a responsibility to something greater than himself; we *all* do.

IVY: Good luck with that.

KAREN: I just can't believe your worldview is that dark.

IVY: You live in Florida.

BARBARA: When are you and Little Charles leaving?

IVY: Weeks, if not days. And his name is Charles.

BARBARA: Are you telling Mom?

IVY: I'm trying to figure that out.

BARBARA: What about your job, your house?

IVY: I've been taking care of myself a lot longer than you've been in charge. Karen, you're going back to Miami, right?

KAREN: Yes.

(Violet descends the stairs.)

IVY: There you go, Barb. You want to know what we're going to do about Mom? Karen and I are leaving. You want to stay and deal with her, that's your decision; if you don't like it, that's your prerogative. But nobody gets to point a finger at me. Nobody.

(Shaky but mainly lucid, Violet enters, knocking softly.)

VIOLET: Hello? Am I interrupting anything?

(Ad-libs: "Not at all," "Come in," etc.)

BARBARA: You had a bath?

VIOLET: Mm-hm.

BARBARA: You need something to eat, or drink?

VIOLET: No.

BARBARA: You want some more coffee?

VIOLET: No, honey, I'm fine.

(Violet sits, exhales. Karen picks up a hand cream from the bedside table, rubs it on her hands.)

You girls all together in this house. Just hearing your voices outside the door gives me a warm feeling. These walls must've heard a lot of secrets.

KAREN: I get embarrassed just thinking about it.

VIOLET: Oh . . . nothing to be embarrassed about. Secret crushes, secret schemes . . . province of teenage girls. I can't imagine anything more delicate, or bittersweet. Some part of you girls I just always identified with . . . no matter how old you get, a woman's hard-pressed to throw off that part of herself.

(To Karen, regarding the hand cream) That smells good.

KAREN: Doesn't it? It's apple. You want some?

VIOLET: Yes, please.

(Karen passes the hand cream to Violet.)

I ever tell you the story of Raymond Qualls? Not much story to it. Boy I had a crush on when I was thirteen or so. Real rough-looking boy, beat-up Levis, messy hair. Terrible underbite. But he had these beautiful cowboy boots, shiny chocolate leather. He was so proud of those boots, you could tell, the way he'd strut around, all arms and elbows, puffed-up and cocksure. I decided I needed to get a girly pair of those same boots and I knew he'd ask me to go steady, convinced myself of it. He'd see me in those boots and say, "Now there's the gal for me." Found the boots in a window downtown and just went crazy: I'd stay up late in bed, praying for those boots, rehearsing the conversation I was going to have with Raymond when he saw me in my boots. Must've asked my momma a hundred times if I could get those boots. "What do you want for Christmas, Vi?" "Momma, I'll give all of it up just for those boots." Bargaining, you know? She started dropping hints about a package under the tree she had wrapped up, about the size of a boot box, real nice wrapping paper. "Now, Vi, don't you cheat and look in there before Christmas morning." Little smile on her face. Christmas morning, I was up like a shot, boy, under the tree, tearing open that box. There was a pair of boots, all right . . . men's work boots, holes in the toes, chewed-up laces, caked in mud and dog shit. Lord, my momma laughed for days.

(Silence.)

BARBARA: Please don't tell me that's the end of that story.

VIOLET: Oh, no. That's the end.

KAREN: You never got the boots?

VIOLET: No, huh-uh.

BARBARA: Okay, well, that's the worst story I ever heard. That makes me wish for a heartwarming claw hammer story.

(Elsewhere in the house: Jean and Steve win the card game with an exclamation of triumph. The players disperse.)

VIOLET: No, no. My momma was a nasty, mean old lady. I suppose that's where I get it from.

(An awkward moment.)

KAREN: You're not nasty-mean. You're our mother and we love you.

VIOLET: Thank you, sweetheart.

(Karen kisses Violet's cheek.)

BARBARA: Hey you all, I need to talk to Mom for a minute.

KAREN: Sure.

(Ivy and Karen exit.)

BARBARA: How's your head?

VIOLET: I'm fine, Barb. Don't worry about that.

BARBARA: I'm sorry.

VIOLET: Please, honey—

BARBARA: No, it's important that I say this. I lost my temper and went too far.

VIOLET: Barbara. The day, the funeral . . . the pills. I was spoiling for a fight and you gave it to me.

BARBARA: So . . . truce?

VIOLET *(Laughs)*: Truce.

BARBARA: What do you want to do?

VIOLET: How do you mean?

BARBARA: Don't you think you should consider a rehab center, or—?

VIOLET: Oh, no. I can't go through that. No, I can do this. I'm pretty sure I can.

BARBARA: Really?

VIOLET: Yes. Well, look, you got rid of my pills, right?

BARBARA: All we could find.

VIOLET: I don't have that many hiding places.

BARBARA: Mom, now, come on.

VIOLET: You wanna search me?

BARBARA: Uh . . . no.

VIOLET: If the pills are gone, I'll be fine. Just take me a few days to get my feet under me.

BARBARA: I can't imagine what all this must be like for you right now. I just want you to know, you're not alone in this.

(No response.)

How can I help?

VIOLET: I don't need help.

BARBARA: I want to help.

VIOLET: I don't need your help.

BARBARA: Mom.

VIOLET: I don't need your *help*. I've gotten myself through some . . . *(Stops, collects herself)* I know how this goes: once all the talking's through, people go back to their own nonsense. I know that. So don't you worry about me. I'll manage. I get by.

(Lights crossfade to the living room where Little Charles watches TV. Ivy enters the room guardedly.)

IVY: Is the coast clear?

LITTLE CHARLES: Never very.

IVY: What are you watching?

LITTLE CHARLES: Television.

IVY: Can I watch it with you?

LITTLE CHARLES: I wish you would.

(She sits beside him on the couch. They watch TV.)

I almost blew it, didn't I?

IVY: Yeah.

LITTLE CHARLES: Are you mad at me?

IVY: Nope.

(They hold hands.)

LITTLE CHARLES: I was trying to be brave.

IVY: I know.

LITTLE CHARLES: I just . . . I want everyone to know that I got what I always wanted. And that means . . . I'm not a loser.

IVY: Hey. Hey.

(He turns to look at her.)

You're my hero.

(He considers this . . . then beams a huge smile. He goes to the electric piano, turns it on.)

LITTLE CHARLES: Come here. You can help me push the pedals.

(She sits beside him on the piano bench.)

I wrote this for you.

(He plays, and quietly sings a gentle but quirky love song. Midway through, Mattie Fae enters from the kitchen, breaking the spell, Charlie in tow.)

MATTIE FAE: Liberace. Get yourself together, we're heading back.

IVY: Are you all staying at   LITTLE CHARLES: Okay . . .
my place?

MATTIE FAE: No, we have to get home and take care of those damn dogs.
IVY: You know you're welcome.

MATTIE FAE *(To Charlie)*: Oh,   CHARLIE: Thanks, Ivy.
look, honey, Little Charles
has got the TV on.

LITTLE CHARLES: No, I was just—
MATTIE FAE *(To Ivy)*: This one watches so much television, it's rotted his brain.
IVY: I'm sure that's not true.
MATTIE FAE *(To Little Charles)*: What was it I caught you watching the other day?

LITTLE CHARLES: I don't   CHARLIE: Mattie Fae—
remember.

MATTIE FAE: You do so remember, some dumb game show about people swapping wives.

LITTLE CHARLES: I don't remember.

MATTIE FAE: You don't remember.

CHARLIE: C'mon, Mattie Fae—

MATTIE FAE: Too bad there isn't a job where they pay you to sit around watching television.

CHARLIE: Mattie Fae, it's been a long day.

MATTIE FAE: I suppose you wouldn't like TV then, not if watching it constituted getting a job.

CHARLIE: Mattie Fae—

MATTIE FAE *(To Ivy)*: Did I tell you he got fired from a *shoe store*?

CHARLIE: Mattie Fae, we're gonna go get in the car right now and go home and if you say one more mean thing to that boy I'm going to kick your fat Irish ass onto the highway. You hear me?

(She wheels on Charlie, stung.)

MATTIE FAE: What the hell did you say?—

CHARLIE: You kids go outside.

(Ivy and Little Charles exit the house.

Barbara, who had started to enter during the previous exchange, stops short, unseen by Charlie or Mattie Fae.)

I don't understand this meanness. I look at you and your sister and the way you talk to people and I don't understand it. I just can't understand why folks can't be respectful of one another. I don't think there's any excuse for it. My family didn't treat each other that way.

MATTIE FAE: Well maybe that's because your family is a—

CHARLIE: You had better not say anything about my family right now. I mean it.

We buried a man today I loved very much. And whatever faults he may have had, he was a good, kind, *decent* person.

And to hear you tear into your own son on a day like today dishonors Beverly's memory.

    We've been married for thirty-eight years. I wouldn't trade them for anything. But if you can't find a generous place in your heart for your own son, we're not going to make it to thirty-nine.

(He leaves. Mattie Fae becomes aware of Barbara.)

BARBARA: I'm sorry, I didn't mean to eavesdrop. I froze.

MATTIE FAE: That's. Do you have a cigarette, hon?

BARBARA: No, I quit years ago.

MATTIE FAE: So did I. It just sounded good to me. Barbara. I thought today at dinner . . . at that horrible dinner, it seemed like . . .

BARBARA: What?

MATTIE FAE: It seemed as if something might be going on between Ivy and Little Charles. Do you know if that's true?

BARBARA: Oh, this is . . . I'm not sure what to say here, it's—

MATTIE FAE: Look, just. Can you tell me if that's true.

BARBARA: Yes. It's true.

MATTIE FAE: Okay. That can't happen.

BARBARA: This is going to be difficult to explain. Um. You know, Ivy and Little Charles have always marched to their own— and obviously, I would expect this to be toughest on *you*—

MATTIE FAE: Barb—?

BARBARA: I think they're very much in love. Or at least they think they are. What's the difference, right? And I'm sure they must be terrified of you and Mom—

MATTIE FAE: Honey—

BARBARA: I realize it's pretty unorthodox for cousins to get together, at least these days—

MATTIE FAE: They're not cousins.

BARBARA: —but believe it or not, it's not as uncommon as you might—

MATTIE FAE: Barbara. Listen to me. They're not cousins.

BARBARA: Beg pardon?

MATTIE FAE: Little Charles is not your cousin. He's your brother. He's your blood brother. He is not your cousin. He is your blood brother. Half-brother. He's your father's child. Which means that he is Ivy's brother. Do you see? Little Charles and Ivy are brother and sister.

BARBARA: No, that's not—no.

MATTIE FAE: Listen—

(Karen and Steve enter.)

BARBARA: No. Go back.

KAREN: We're just going to—

BARBARA: Go back into the kitchen. Now! Just . . . everyone stay in the kitchen!

(Karen and Steve retreat to the kitchen.)

No, that's wrong. You. Okay, well this may be—are you sure?

MATTIE FAE: Yes.

BARBARA: You and Dad.

MATTIE FAE: Yes.

BARBARA: Who knows this?

MATTIE FAE: I do. And you do.

BARBARA: Uncle Charlie doesn't suspect.

MATTIE FAE: We've never discussed it.

BARBARA: What?!

MATTIE FAE: We've never discussed it. Okay?

BARBARA: Did Dad know?

(Mattie Fae nods.)

MATTIE FAE: Y'know, I'm not proud of this.

BARBARA: *Really.* You people amaze me. What, were you drunk? Was this just some—?

MATTIE FAE: I wasn't drunk, no. Maybe it's hard for you to believe, looking at me, knowing me the way you do, all these years. I know to you, I'm just your old fat Aunt Mattie Fae. But I'm more than that, sweetheart . . . there's more to me than that.

Charlie's right, of course. As usual. I don't know why Little Charles is such a disappointment to me. Maybe he . . . well, I don't know why. I guess I'm disappointed *for* him, more than anything.

I made a mistake, a long time ago. Well, okay. Fair enough. I've paid for it. But the mistake ends here.

BARBARA: If Ivy found out about this, it would destroy her.

MATTIE FAE: *I'm* sure as hell not gonna tell her. You have to find a way to stop it. You have to put a stop to it.

BARBARA: Why me?

MATTIE FAE: You said you were running things.

SCENE 2

Giggling from the kitchen. Jean and Steve quietly scamper from the kitchen into the dining room, sharing a joint. She wears a knee-length T-shirt and white socks; he wears sweatpants and a sleeve-less T-shirt.

The rest of the house is sleeping. Karen sleeps in the living room on the unfolded hide-a-bed. Bill sleeps on the mattress in the study.

STEVE: Shhh . . .

(Jean snort-laughs.)

You're gonna get me busted, you.

JEAN: I thought you weren't doing anything wrong.

STEVE: We're not, but some folks may not be crazy about me smoking pot with a girl born during the Clinton administration.

JEAN: First Bush.

STEVE: Great. Stop talking about your bush, all right? You're gonna get me hot and bothered—

JEAN *(Laughing)*: You are sick—

STEVE: —and I won't be able to control myself.

JEAN: God, you weren't kidding, this stuff is strong.

STEVE: Florida, baby. Number one industry.

JEAN: Who cares?

STEVE: Number one, by far. You want a shotgun?

JEAN: Huh?

STEVE: You don't know what a shotgun is?

JEAN: I know what a shotgun is.

STEVE: Not that kind of shotgun—here. Just put your lips right next to mine and you inhale while I exhale.

JEAN: Okay.

(He puts the joint in his mouth, lit end first. Their lips nearly touch as he blows marijuana smoke into her mouth in a steady stream. She nearly chokes.)

STEVE: Hold it. Don't let it out.

(She finally gasps, exhales, coughs.)

JEAN: Whoa.

STEVE: That's a kick, huh?

JEAN: Whoa, shit, man.

STEVE *(Laughs)*: That's what I'm talkin' about.

JEAN: Whoa, Jesus—

(She takes an off-balance step, sways. He catches her, holds her.)

STEVE: Careful, now—

JEAN: Oh, man, what a head rush.

STEVE: You okay? You're not passing out on me, are you?

JEAN: No, I'm cool. Oh God . . . *(Coughs deeply)* I really feel that in my chest.

(He reaches for her breasts.)

STEVE: Here, let me feel.

(Unperturbed, she pushes him away.)

JEAN: You're just an old perv.

STEVE: No shit. Christ, you got a great set. *How* old are you?

JEAN: I'm fifteen, perv.

STEVE: Show 'em to me.

JEAN: No, perv.

STEVE: Shhh. Yeah, show 'em to me. I won't look.

JEAN: If you won't look, there's no point in showing them to you.

STEVE: Okay, okay, I'll look then.

JEAN *(Dumb guy voice)*: "Lemme look at your tits, little girl—"

STEVE: C'mon, we're partners!

JEAN: No!

STEVE: Aren't we amazing card partners?

JEAN: Forget it!

STEVE: I'll show you mine if you show me yours.

JEAN: I don't want to see yours.

STEVE: You ever seen one?

JEAN: Yes.

STEVE: No, you haven't.

JEAN: Yes, I have. I'm not a virgin.

STEVE: You're not?

JEAN: Not technically. Well, no *technically*, I am. I mean not theoretically.

STEVE: That changes everything.

(He moves in close to her.)

JEAN: What are you doing?

STEVE: Nothing.

JEAN: You're gonna get us both in trouble.

STEVE: I'm white and over thirty. I don't get in trouble.

(He turns off the light. Total darkness.)

JEAN: Hey . . .

STEVE: Shhh . . .

(Moaning, heavy breathing from Steve, in the dark. The over-head light clicks on. Johnna stands in the dining-room entry-way, brandishing a cast-iron skillet. Jean and Steve, clothes in disarray, separate.)

JEAN: Oh my God . . .

STEVE: Ho, fuck!

(Johnna approaches Steve.)

Hold up there, lady, you don't know what you're—

(Johnna swings the skillet, barely missing Steve's nose.)

Hey, goddamn it, careful—

(He reaches for the skillet. She swings again and smacks his knuckles.)

Ow, goddamn—!

(He grimaces, holds his hand in pain. She wades in with a strong swing and connects squarely with his forehead. Steve goes down. Johnna stands above him, arm cocked, watching for a recovery, but he does not attempt it.

Elsewhere in the house: Bill, Barbara and Karen wake in their different locations, head to the dining room.

Karen sees Steve on the floor and screams:)

KAREN: What happened?!

(Johnna and Jean share a look. Karen goes to Steve, props him up.)

Steve, what happened?!

(He groans.)

Tell me what happened.
JOHNNA: He was messing with Jean—
KAREN: Honey, you're bleeding, are you okay?

(He groans again, tries to stand.
Now Bill and Barbara enter the dining room, both in their night clothes.)

BARBARA: Jean, what are you doing up? What's going on—?
JEAN: We were, I don't know—

BARBARA: Who was? Talk to me, are you all right?
JEAN: Yeah, I'm fine.

BILL: What happened to him? Do I need to call a doctor?
KAREN: I don't know.

BARBARA: Johnna, what's going on?
JOHNNA: He was messing with Jean. So I tuned him up.

BARBARA: "Messing with," what do you mean, "messing with"?

BILL: What . . . what's that mean?

JOHNNA: He was kissing her and grabbing her.

(This information settles in . . .
Then Barbara attacks Steve, who has by now gotten to his feet. Ad-libs. Karen gets between them. Bill grabs Barbara from behind, tries to pull her away. Ad-libs.)

BARBARA: I'll murder you, you prick!

BILL *(To Karen)*: Get him out of here!

STEVE: I didn't do anything!—

JEAN: Mom, stop it!

KAREN: Settle down!—

BILL: Get back in the living room!—

BARBARA: You know how old that girl is?!

STEVE *(To Jean)*: Tell them I didn't do anything!—

BARBARA: She's fourteen years old!—

JEAN: Mom!

STEVE: She said she was fifteen!

BARBARA: Are you out of your goddamn mind?

KAREN: Barbara, just back off!

(Karen manages to push Steve out of the dining room, into the living room. During the following, they get dressed and pack their bags.

Barbara, Bill, Jean and Johnna remain in the dining room.)

BARBARA: Oh my God! Do you fucking believe that crazy prick?!

BILL: I know, I know, settle down.

BARBARA: "Settle down," the son-of-a-bitch is a goddamn sociopath! What the fuck is going on?

BILL *(To Jean)*: Are you okay?

JEAN: Yes, I'm okay, what is the *matter* with you?

BARBARA: With *us*?

JEAN: Will you please stop freaking out?

BILL: Why don't you start at the beginning?

BARBARA: What are you doing out of bed?

BILL: Please, sweetheart, we need to know what went on here.

JEAN: Nothing "went on." Can we just not make a federal case out of everything? I couldn't sleep, I came to the kitchen for a drink, he came in . . . end of story.

| BARBARA: That's not the end of the story. | BILL: That's not the end of the story. |

JEAN: We smoked pot, all right? We smoked a little pot, and we were goofing around, and then everything just went haywire.

BARBARA: What have I told you about smoking that shit?! What did I say?	BILL: Then Johnna just chose to attack him with a frying pan? I don't think so.

JEAN: Look at you two, you're both so ridiculous. It's no big deal, nothing happened.

BILL: We're concerned about you.

JEAN: No, you're not. You just want to know who to punish.

BARBARA: Stop it—

JEAN: You can't tell the difference between the good guys and the bad guys, so you want me to sort it all out for you—

BARBARA: You know what, skip the lecture. Just tell me what he did!

JEAN: He didn't do anything! Even if he did, what's the big deal?

BILL: The big deal, Jean, is that you're fourteen years old.

JEAN: Which is only a few years younger than you like 'em.

(Barbara slaps Jean; Jean bursts into tears.)

I hate you!

BARBARA: Yeah, I hate you too, you little freak!

(Jean tries to exit. Bill grabs her.)

BILL: Jean—

JEAN: Let me go!

(Jean pulls free, runs off.)

BILL *(To Barbara)*: What's the matter with you?

(Bill exits, pursuing Jean.)

JOHNNA: Excuse me.

(Johnna exits, returns to her attic room. Barbara regains some composure, moves into the living room. Steve has by now dressed and exited, carrying suitcases. Karen is pulling on a sweatshirt, grabbing a few leftover items, restoring the hide-a-bed.)

KAREN: I can do without a speech.

BARBARA: I beg your pardon?

KAREN: I'm leaving. *We're* leaving. Back to Florida, tonight, *now*. Me and Steve, together. You want to give me some grief about that?

BARBARA: Now wait just a goddamn—

KAREN: You better find out from Jean just exactly what went on in there before you start pointing fingers, that's all I'm saying. 'Cause I doubt Jean's exactly blameless in all this. And I'm not *blaming* her. Just because I said she's not blameless, that doesn't mean I've *blamed* her. I'm saying she might share in the responsibility. You understand me?

I know Steve should know better than Jean, that she's only fourteen. My point is, it's not cut and dried, black and white, good and bad. It lives where everything lives: somewhere in the middle. Where everything lives, where all the rest of us live, *everyone but you.*

BARBARA: Karen—

KAREN: I'm not defending him. He's not perfect. Just like all the rest of us, down here in the muck. I'm no angel myself. I've done some things I'm not proud of. Things you'll never know about. Know what? I may even have to do some things I'm not proud of *again*. 'Cause sometimes life puts you in a corner that way. And I am a human being, after all.

Anyway you have your own hash to settle. Before you start making speeches to the rest of us.

BARBARA: Right . . .

KAREN: Come January . . . I'll be in Belize. Doesn't that sound nice?

(Karen exits, rolling her suitcase behind her. Bill enters.)

BILL: I'm taking Jean with me. We're heading back.

BARBARA: Fine.

BILL: She's too much for you right now.

BARBARA: Okay.

BILL: I'm sure you'll blame me for all this.

BARBARA: Yeah, well . . . *(Beat)* I fail. As a sister, as a mother, as a wife. I fail.

BILL: No, you don't.

BARBARA: No? I've physically attacked Mom and Jean in the space of about nine hours. Stick around here much longer and I'll cut off your penis.

BILL: That's not funny.

BARBARA: I can't make it up to Jean right now. She's just going to have to wait until I come back to Boulder.

BILL: You and Jean have about forty years left to fight and make up.

BARBARA *(Confused)*: Why, what happens in forty years?

BILL: You die.

BARBARA: Oh, right.

BILL: I mean—

BARBARA: No. Right.

BILL: If you're lucky.

BARBARA: Says you.

BILL: If *we're* lucky.

(Pause.)

BARBARA: You're never coming back to me, are you, Bill?

BILL: Never say never, but . . .

BARBARA: But no.

BILL: But no.

BARBARA: Even if things don't work out with you and Marsha.

BILL: Cindy.

BARBARA: Cindy.

BILL: Right. Even if things don't work out.

BARBARA: And I'm never really going to understand why, am I?

(Bill struggles . . . it seems as if he might say something more, but then:)

BILL: Probably not.

(Silence. Bill heads for the door. Barbara watches him go and sobs.)

BARBARA: I love you . . . I love you . . .

(He stands for a moment, his back to her. He exits.
Barbara stands, alone.)

SCENE 3

The study: Barbara and Johnna, in the same positions as Beverly and Johnna in the Prologue.
Barbara's had a few. She nurses a glass of whiskey.

BARBARA: One of the last times I spoke with my father, we were talking about . . . I don't know, the state of the world, some-thing . . . and he said, "You know, this country was always pretty much a whorehouse, but at least it used to have some promise. Now it's just a shithole." And I think now maybe he was talking about something else, something more spe-cific, something more personal to him . . . this house? This family? His marriage? Himself? I don't know. But there was something sad in his voice—or no, not sad, he always sounded sad—something more hopeless than that. As if it had already happened. As if whatever was disappearing had already disappeared. As if it was too late. As if it was already over. And no one saw it go. This country, this experiment, America, this hubris: what a lament, if no one saw it go. Here today, gone tomorrow. *(Beat)* Dissipation is actually much worse than cataclysm.

JOHNNA: Mrs. Fordham, are you firing me?

BARBARA: Barbara. No, no. Oh, no. Far from it. I'm owning up to my own shitty behavior. And I'm giving you the opportunity to quit. I mean . . . there's work. And then there's *work.* And after all . . . I'm here. Look around. No one else is here. I mean, am I here, or am I here? I'm not saying your services aren't necessary. I just mean: *I'm* still here, goddamn it.

JOHNNA: I'm prepared to stay. I'm familiar with this job. I can do this job. I don't do it for you or Mrs. Weston. Or even for Mr. Weston. Right? I do it for me.

BARBARA: Why?

JOHNNA: I need the work.

(Barbara finishes her glass of whiskey.)

BARBARA: Johnna . . . what did my father say to you?

(Pause.)

JOHNNA: He talked a lot about his daughters . . . his three daughters, and his granddaughter. That was his joy.

BARBARA: Thank you. That makes me feel better. Knowing that you can lie. *(Beat)* I want you to stay on. Don't worry about your salary. I'll take care of it.

(Johnna nods, exits. Barbara refills her whiskey glass.)

(To herself) I'm still here, goddamn it.

SCENE 4

For the first time since the shades were removed from the windows, the house is seen in morning light.

Barbara and Sheriff Gilbeau stand in the living room.

BARBARA: Everyone just . . . vanished.

SHERIFF GILBEAU: You were the one I wanted to talk to.

BARBARA: 'Kay. Sit down. Do you want some coffee?

SHERIFF GILBEAU: No, thanks.

BARBARA: God, Deon, you look really good. You really . . . filled out. *Nicely*, I mean. You just look great.

SHERIFF GILBEAU: Thanks.

BARBARA: How 'bout me, don't I look good?

SHERIFF GILBEAU: Yes, sorry, yes. You look great, too, just great.

BARBARA: Did you want some coffee?

SHERIFF GILBEAU: Uh. No. No, thank you.

BARBARA: And you're the sheriff. Of all things. That's ironic.

SHERIFF GILBEAU: Why is that ironic?

BARBARA: It's not. It's incongruous. I think I misused "ironic." Oh, if my husband could hear *that*. Well, fuck him. No, but it is, "incongruous."

SHERIFF GILBEAU: Why's it incongruous?

BARBARA: Because of your, because of your . . . your dad.

SHERIFF GILBEAU: Oh, I see, yeah.

BARBARA: Is he still alive?

SHERIFF GILBEAU: Yeah, after a fashion. He has Alzheimer's.

BARBARA: Oh. That's awful.

SHERIFF GILBEAU: He's in a home over in Nowata.

BARBARA: I'm sorry to hear that. That's just. Married? You're married? Wow. Hot flash. I'm sorry, did you want some coffee? I asked you that already. You're married.

SHERIFF GILBEAU: Divorced.

BARBARA: Join the club.

SHERIFF GILBEAU: Really?

BARBARA: I mean, I'm joining your club. I mean looks like I'll be joining your, your club.

SHERIFF GILBEAU: Sorry to hear that.

BARBARA: Have kids?

SHERIFF GILBEAU: Three daughters.

BARBARA: Uh-huh. Look at that.

SHERIFF GILBEAU: Right, no, I can't tell you—

BARBARA: Three daughters, that's—

SHERIFF GILBEAU: —how many times I've thought about the Weston sisters over the years.

BARBARA: The Weston sisters. Been a while since I heard that. Sounds like a singing group.

SHERIFF GILBEAU: Yeah, I guess.

BARBARA: "Ladies and gentlemen . . . The Agitated Weston Sisters."

SHERIFF GILBEAU: Is your husband still here?

BARBARA: No, he left a few days ago. A week ago? Two weeks ago. Two weeks ago? Back to Colorado, with my daughter. With Jean.

SHERIFF GILBEAU: She seemed real sweet.

BARBARA: Ah, she's a nymphomaniac.

SHERIFF GILBEAU: Really.

BARBARA: "*Jean*." That's a stupid name.

SHERIFF GILBEAU: I like it.

BARBARA: You know why we named her that? Bill's a big Jean Seberg fan. Now *that's* ironic.

SHERIFF GILBEAU: I don't get it.

BARBARA: Jean Seberg killed herself. With a massive over-blah of . . . blah-biturates.

SHERIFF GILBEAU: Oh.

BARBARA: So.

(Silence.)

SHERIFF GILBEAU: Barbara? Are you okay?

BARBARA *(Softly)*: I'm fine. Just got the Plains.

SHERIFF GILBEAU: I thought . . . I thought if you were going to be staying here a while we might get some lunch someday. Catch up? Been a long time.

BARBARA: Mm.

SHERIFF GILBEAU: Would you like to get some lunch someday?

BARBARA: Mm-hm.

SHERIFF GILBEAU: The other reason I came. I got a call from a woman named Chitra Naidu, who runs the Country Squire Motel. She was throwing out some old newspapers and she saw a photo of Mr. Weston that ran with his obituary. And she recognized him as the man who stayed in Room 17 for two nights, the first two nights of his absence. *(Beat)* She said he checked in and she didn't see him again until he checked out. He made no phone calls. She has no way of telling if he received any phone calls. But I can have a check run on the line to find out if he did.

BARBARA: Do you have a . . . cigarette?

SHERIFF GILBEAU: Yeah, sure. *(Fishes for a cigarette)* I can check with the phone company, is what I mean.

(He lights her smoke.)

BARBARA: That's not. No one knew where he was. I suppose he was, what . . . just trying to build up the courage to jump in the water, I guess.

SHERIFF GILBEAU: Or overcoming the courage not to.

BARBARA: Right? I don't follow that, but it doesn't matter.

SHERIFF GILBEAU: In any case. I thought you should know.

(A sad, still moment.)

So . . . I can call you sometime? About having lunch?

BARBARA: Come here.

SHERIFF GILBEAU: Barbara?

BARBARA: Sh. Come here . . .

(He does not.)

Come here . . .

(He does. She touches his face.)

Sweet . . .

SHERIFF GILBEAU: Barbara . . .
BARBARA: Mm . . . just . . . touches . . .

(She kisses him. He begins to take her arms but she moves away.)

SHERIFF GILBEAU: Barbara.
BARBARA: I'm . . .
SHERIFF GILBEAU: I'm sorry?
BARBARA: I . . .
SHERIFF GILBEAU: Barbara? Barbara, did you say something?
BARBARA: I've forgotten what I look like.

SCENE 5

Barbara, still wearing her nightgown, and Ivy, in the dining room.
The house has taken on a ghostly cast.
    Elsewhere in the house: Johnna prepares dinner in the kitchen.

IVY: Is she clean?
BARBARA: Clean-ish.
IVY: So she's not clean.
BARBARA: The woman's got brain-damage, dummy. If you think
    I'm going to strip-search her every time she slurs a word—
IVY: You know the difference.
BARBARA: She's moderately clean.
IVY: "Moderately"?
BARBARA: You don't like "moderately"? Then let's say tolerably.
IVY: Is she clean, or not?

BARBARA: Back off. We're trying to get by here, okay?

IVY: I'm nervous.

BARBARA: Why? Oh, Christ, Ivy, not tonight.

IVY: Why not?

BARBARA: We're only just now settling into some kind of rhythm around here. Now you come in here with your little *issues*—

IVY: I have to tell her, don't I? We're leaving for New York tomorrow.

BARBARA: That's not a good idea.

IVY: "A good idea."

BARBARA: For you and Little Charles to take this thing any further.

IVY: Where is this coming from?

BARBARA: I just got to thinking about it, and I think it's a little weird, that's all.

IVY: It's not up to you.

BARBARA: Lot of fish in the sea. Surely you can rule out the one single man in the world you're related to.

IVY: I happen to love the man I'm related—

BARBARA: *Fuck love*, what a crock of shit. People can convince themselves they love a painted rock.

(Johnna brings food from the kitchen.)

Looks great. What is it?

JOHNNA: Catfish.

BARBARA: Bottom feeders, my favorite.

(Johnna retires to the kitchen.
Violet enters from the second-floor hallway, heads slowly for the dining room.)

IVY: You think I shouldn't tell her.

BARBARA: You should rethink the whole proposition. New York City is a ridiculous idea. You're almost fifty years old,

Ivy, you can't go to New York, you'll break a hip. Eat your catfish.

IVY: You're infuriating.

BARBARA: I ain't the one fuckin' my cousin.

IVY: I have lived in this town, year in and year out, hoping against hope someone would come into my life—

BARBARA: Don't get all Carson McCullers on me. Now wipe that tragic look off your face and eat some catfish.

IVY: Who are you to speak to me like this?

(Violet enters the dining room.)

BARBARA: Howdy, Mom.

VIOLET: What's howdy about it?

BARBARA: Look, catfish.

VIOLET: Catfish.

BARBARA *(Calling off)*: Johnna! *(To Violet)* You hungry?

VIOLET: Ivy, you should smile. Like me.

(Johnna enters.)

BARBARA: Mom needs her dinner, please.

(Johnna exits.)

VIOLET: I'm not hungry.

BARBARA: You haven't eaten anything today. You didn't eat anything yesterday.

VIOLET: I'm not hungry.

BARBARA: You're eating. You do what I say. Everyone do what I say.

IVY: May I ask why neither of you is dressed?

BARBARA: What is it with you?

VIOLET: Yeah.

BARBARA: We're dressed. We're not sitting here naked, are we? Or did you want us to dress up?

VIOLET: Right, 'cause you're coming over for fish.

BARBARA: Right, 'cause you're coming over for fish we're supposed to dress up.

(*Johnna reenters with two plates of food.*)

JOHNNA: I'll eat in my room.

BARBARA: That's fine, thank you.

(*Johnna exits with her plate of food.*)

(*To Violet*) Eat.

VIOLET: No.

BARBARA: Eat it. Mom? Eat it.

VIOLET: No.

BARBARA: Eat it, you fucker. Eat that catfish.

VIOLET: Go to hell!

BARBARA: That doesn't cut any fucking ice with me. Now eat that fucking fish.

IVY: Mom. I have something to talk to you about.

BARBARA: No, you don't.

IVY: Barbara—

BARBARA: No, you don't. Shut up. Shut the fuck up.

IVY: Please—

VIOLET: What's to talk about?

IVY: Mom—

BARBARA: Forget it. Mom? Eat that fucking fish.

VIOLET: I'm not hungry.

BARBARA: Eat it.

VIOLET: NO!

IVY: Mom, I need to—!

VIOLET: NO!

IVY: Mom!

BARBARA: EAT THE FISH, BITCH!

IVY: Mom, please!

VIOLET: Barbara . . . !

BARBARA: Okay, fuck it, do what you want.

IVY: I have to tell you something.

BARBARA: Ivy's a lesbian.

VIOLET: What?

IVY: Barbara—

VIOLET: No, you're not.

IVY: No, I'm not—

BARBARA: Yes, you are. Did you eat your fish?

IVY: Barbara, stop it!

BARBARA: Eat your fish.

IVY: Barbara!

BARBARA: Eat your fish.

VIOLET: Barbara, quiet now—

IVY: Mom, please, this is important—

BARBARA: Eatyourfisheatyourfisheatyourfish—

(Ivy hurls her plate of food, smashes it.)

What the fuck—

IVY: I have something to say!

BARBARA: Are we breaking shit?

(Barbara takes a vase from the sideboard, smashes it.)

'Cause I can break shit—

(Violet throws her plate, smashes it.)

See, we can all break shit.

IVY: Charles and I—

BARBARA: You don't want to break shit with *me*, muthah-fuckah!

IVY: Charles and I—

BARBARA: Johnna?! Little spill in here!

IVY: Barbara, stop it! Mom, Charles and I—

BARBARA: Little Charles—

IVY: Charles and I—
BARBARA: Little Charles—
IVY: Charles and I—
BARBARA: Little Charles—
IVY: Charles and I—
BARBARA: Little Charles—
IVY: Barbara—
BARBARA: You have to say "Little Charles" or she won't know who you're talking about.
IVY: Little Charles and I . . .

(Barbara relents. Ivy will finally get to say the words.)

Little Charles and I are—
VIOLET: Little Charles and you are brother and sister. I know that.
BARBARA: Oh . . . Mom.
IVY: What? *No*, listen to me, Little Charles—
VIOLET: I've always known that. I told you, no one slips anything by me.
IVY: *Mom—*
BARBARA: Don't listen to her.
VIOLET: I knew the whole time Bev and Mattie Fae were carrying on. Charlie shoulda known too, if he wasn't smoking all that grass.
BARBARA: It's the pills talking.
VIOLET: Pills can't talk.
IVY: Wait . . .
VIOLET: Your father tore himself up over it, for thirty some-odd years, but Beverly wouldn't have been Beverly if he didn't have plenty to brood about.
IVY: Mom, what are you . . . ?
BARBARA: Oh, honey . . .
VIOLET: It's better you girls know now, though, now you're older. Never know when someone might need a kidney. Better if everyone knows the truth.

IVY: Oh my God . . .

VIOLET: Though I can't see the benefit in Little Charles ever knowing, break his little heart. *(Tell Ivy)* Tell me though, honey: how'd *you* find out?

(Ivy looks from Violet to Barbara . . . suddenly lurches away from the table, knocking over her chair.)

BARBARA: Ivy?

IVY: Why did you tell me? Why in God's name did you tell me this?

VIOLET: Hey, what do *you* care?

IVY: You're monsters.

VIOLET: Come on now—

IVY: Picking the bones of the rest of us—

VIOLET: You crazy nut.

IVY: Monsters.

VIOLET: Who's the injured party here?

(Ivy staggers out of the dining room, into the living room. Barbara pursues her.)

BARBARA: Ivy, listen—

IVY: Leave me alone!

BARBARA: Honey—

IVY: I won't let you do this to me!

BARBARA: When Mattie Fae told me, I didn't know what to do—

IVY: I won't let you change my story!

(Ivy exits. Barbara chases after her and catches her on the front porch.)

BARBARA: Goddamn it, listen to me: I tried to protect you—

IVY: We'll go anyway. We'll still go away, and you will never see me again.

BARBARA: Don't leave me like this.

IVY: *You will never see me again.*

BARBARA: This is not my fault. I didn't tell you, *Mom* told you. It wasn't me, it was *Mom.*

IVY: There's no difference.

(Ivy exits. Barbara reenters the house. She finds Violet lighting a cigarette in the living room.)

VIOLET: You know well's I do, we couldn't let Ivy run off with Little Charles. Just wouldn't be right. Ivy's place is right here.

BARBARA: She says she's leaving anyway.

VIOLET: Nah. She won't go. She's a sweet girl, Ivy, and I love her to death. But she isn't strong. Not like you. Or me.

BARBARA: Right. *(Beat)* You've known about Daddy and Mattie Fae all these years.

VIOLET: Oh, sure. I never told them I knew. But your father knew. He knew I knew. He always knew I knew. But we never talked about it. I chose the higher ground.

BARBARA: Right.

VIOLET: Now if I'd had the chance, there at the end, I would've told him, "I hope this isn't about Little Charles, 'cause you know I know all about that." If I'd reached him at the motel, I would've said, "You'd be better off if you quit sulking about this ancient history. And anyway, just 'cause you feel cast down doesn't let you off the hook."

BARBARA: If you had reached him at the motel.

VIOLET: I *called* the motel, the Country Squire Motel—

BARBARA: —the Country Squire Motel, right—

VIOLET: —but it was too late, he must've already checked out. I called over there on Monday, after I got into that safety deposit box. I told you I had to wait until Monday morning for the bank to open so I could get into that safety deposit box. I should've called him sooner, I guess, should've called the police, or Ivy, someone. But Beverly and I had an arrangement. You have to understand, for people like your father and me, who never had any money, ever, as kids, people from our generation, that money is important.

BARBARA: How'd you know where he was?

VIOLET: He left a note. Said I could call him at the Country Squire Motel. And I did, I did call him, called him on Monday.

BARBARA: After you got into your safety deposit box.

VIOLET: We had an arrangement.

BARBARA: If you could've stopped Daddy from killing himself, you wouldn't have *needed* to get into your safety deposit box.

VIOLET: Well, hindsight's twenty-twenty, isn't it.

BARBARA: Did the note say Daddy was going to kill himself?

(No response.)

Mom?

VIOLET: If I'd had my wits about me, I might've done it different. But I was, your father and me both, we were . . .

BARBARA: You were both fucked-up. *(Beat)* You were fucked-up. *(Beat)* You're fucked-up.

VIOLET: You had better understand this, you smug little ingrate, there is at least one reason Beverly killed himself and that's *you*. Think there's any way he would've done what he did if you were still here? No, just him and me, here in this house, in the dark, left to just ourselves, abandoned, wasted lifetimes devoted to your care and comfort. So stick that knife of judgment in me, go ahead, but make no mistake, his blood is just as much on your hands as it is on mine.

(No response. Violet enters the study. Barbara follows.)

He did this, though; this was his doing, not ours. Can you imagine anything more cruel, to make *me* responsible? And why, just to weaken me, just to make me prove my character? So no, I waited, I waited so I could get my hands on that safety deposit box, but I would have waited anyway. You want to show who's stronger, Bev? Nobody is stronger than me, goddamn it. When nothing is left, when everything is gone and disappeared, I'll be here. Who's stronger now, you son-of-a-bitch?!

BARBARA: No, you're right, Mom. You're the strong one.

(Barbara kisses her mother . . . exits the study, returns to the living room. Violet calls after her.)

VIOLET: Barbara?

(Barbara grabs her purse, digs out rental car keys.)

Barbara?

(Barbara stands, listens to her mother.)

Barbara, please.

(Barbara exits the house.)

Please, Barbara. *Please.*

(Violet shuffles into the living room.)

Barbara? You in here?

(She crosses to the dining room.)

Ivy? Ivy, you here? Barb?

(She crosses to the kitchen.)

Barb? Ivy?

(She turns in a circle, disoriented, panicked. She crosses to the study.)

Bev?

(She reenters the living room, stumbles to the stereo, puts on Clapton . . . stares at the turntable as the album spins . . . attacks the record player, rakes the needle across the album. She looks around, terrified, disoriented.)

Johnna?!

(She reels to the stairway, crawls up the stairs on all fours.)

Johnna, Johnna, Johnna . . .

(She arrives on the second floor. Johnna puts her plate of food aside and turns toward the stairs. Violet, on all fours, continues up the stairs to the attic. She arrives in Johnna's room. She scrabbles into Johnna's lap. Johnna holds Violet's head, smoothes her hair, rocks her.)

And then you're gone, and Beverly, and then you're gone, and Barbara, and then you're gone, and then you're gone, and then you're gone—

(Johnna quietly sings to Violet.)

JOHNNA: "This is the way the world ends, this is the way the world ends, this is the way the world ends . . ."

VIOLET: —and then you're gone, and then you're gone, and then you're gone, and then you're gone—

(Blackout.)

END OF PLAY

TRACY LETTS is the author of *Killer Joe*, *Bug* and *Man from Nebraska*, which was a finalist for the 2004 Pulitzer Prize for Drama. He is a member of the Steppenwolf Theatre Company, where *August: Osage County* premiered. His latest play is *Superior Donuts*.